# Wetlands Protection:
# The Role of
# Economics

# Wetlands Protection: The Role of Economics

Paul F. Scodari

Environmental Law Institute
Washington, D.C.

**Library of Congress Cataloging-in-Publication Data**

Scodari, Paul, F., 1957-
    Wetlands protection: the role of economics/Paul F. Scodari.
    p.   cm.—(ELI monograph series)
    "February 1990."
    Includes bibliographical references.
    ISBN 0-911937-32-3: $28.00
    1. Wetlands—Economic aspects—United States. 2. Wetlands—Law and legislation—Economic aspects—United States. I. Environmental Law Institute. II. Title. III. Series: ELI monograph series
(Unnumbered)
HD1671.U5S36   1990                          89-71414
333.91'816'0973—dc20                         CIP

# Contents

# Foreword

*Wetlands Protection: The Role of Economics* is a report by the Environmental Law Institute on how economic analysis can be used to strengthen wetlands protection efforts. One of the great problems in environmental policy is how to protect undervalued natural resources such as wetlands from exploitation by unwise development. Despite the mounting evidence of their high value, wetlands in the United States continue to be lost at the rate of 200,000 to 400,000 acres a year to agriculture, urban development, vacation homes, and water resource development projects.

This report concludes that current economic assessment approaches do not meaningfully account for the wetland values being destroyed by development. But it offers hope by pointing out opportunities to improve those approaches.

Much wetland destruction results from government water resource development projects. By law, these projects can be funded only after publication of economic analyses (cost-benefit studies). For too long, though, these economic analyses on barge canals and dams have undercounted environmental costs and have inflated immediate economic benefits. Environmental reformers urge that economic analyses of public works projects should identify and incorporate values for the hidden costs of development.

This report suggests limited methodological reforms that will improve accounting on wetlands projects. However, these suggested reforms will not make a significant difference in catching the uncounted benefits lost through wetlands conversion. Under the conventional economics respected by the courts in reviewing expert evidence taken at trial, these incremental reforms are as much as can be expected at this time without legislative changes.

But economics is not a static field. Congress changes the rules and mandates new arrangements in economics just as it does in other fields of human enterprise. For instance, Congress changed the rules concerning the use of economics for valuing natural resource damages when it passed the Comprehensive Environmental Response, Compensation, and Liability Act (CERCLA) in 1980.

CERCLA's requirements for valuing natural resource damages were open to a variety of plausible interpretations. In a seminal study for the National Oceanic and Atmospheric Administration in 1982, ELI staffers built a framework for a rational analysis of damages which was extended and refined in articles appearing in professional journals. Articles by staff attorneys explored the rules of evidence, statute of limitations, and legal standing. ELI's work was cited in the July 1989 District of Columbia Circuit Court decision on natural resource damages.

ELI's eight years of experience in breathing life into the natural resource damages concept have underscored the dynamic nature of environmental economics. Chapter Five of *Wetlands Protection* traces the relevance of the natural resource damages experience to the emerging field of wetlands valuation. If wetlands protection advocates want to enlist economics as an aid in their efforts, they must look to Congress, which has the power to change the rules on how economics is used to evaluate development damage to natural resources. *Wetlands Protection* recommends several such changes.

The report also offers recommendations on better scientific efforts in wetlands protection. ELI recommends a major effort by scientists in both government and the private sector to improve biological and ecological data bases. Scientists need to be able to tell us more about how wetlands function and what services might be affected by cumulative water developments. These effects must be segregated, identified, and analyzed before economic analysis can be effectively applied to measure the social costs of proposed wetland developments. Not even the best economic formula on resource valuation will be of service if scientific knowledge on wetland goods and services is not available.

A further recommendation concerns the need for improved communication between wetland scientists and economists. Very few institutional arrangements facilitate this interaction. A starting point in the process might be the establishment of ongoing dialogue groups, which would include core groups of scientists and economists working on wetland issues. Interdisciplinary efforts are essential.

To create this monograph, ELI drew on the resources of its wetlands program and economics staff. ELI's wetlands program is a uniquely effective combination of research, education, and technical assistance efforts. In-house expertise has been expanded by the Institute's affiliation with the National Wetlands Technical Council, made up of the country's leading wetlands scientists. ELI's wetlands work is widely used by the states and by the U.S. Environmental Protection Agency, which seeks analytical support from our research division and training courses on wetlands enforcement from our continuing education program. ELI's *National Wetlands Newsletter* is a respected journal that has been a communications medium for wetlands scientists, policymakers, conservationists, and managers nationwide since 1978. Basic reference texts, such as *Our National Wetlands*

*Heritage* (now in its fifth printing), *Wetlands of the Chesapeake*, and *Non-Tidal Wetlands Protection*, form another component of the Institute's wetlands program. The program has learned that economic analysis can be a powerful factor in shaping wetlands policy.

ELI's economics program works to achieve economic efficiency in the pursuit of environmental improvement. Since its inception in 1976, it has created a unique niche, specializing in the interface between economics and law. EPA and other agencies have called on ELI for research on methods for structuring and implementing laws that will achieve environmental goals at the lowest possible cost to society.

ELI's economics program relies on a three-part research agenda. The first part focuses on identifying the various impediments to economic efficiency, be they statutory, institutional, regulatory, administrative, or methodological. The second part focuses on developing and summarizing data on the costs and benefits of environmental programs, highlighting potential inefficiencies. This monograph, like much of ELI's work, focuses primarily on the third part: identifying, developing, and implementing reforms that can make environmental policy more efficient.

This integrated research effort drew the support of the Mary Flagler Cary Trust, whose Trustees are dedicated to protecting threatened coastal areas. Through the good offices of the Cary Trust, ELI had the opportunity to work with The Conservancy in Naples, Florida, in its ongoing effort to protect Collier County wetlands on the border of the Everglades. At the end of the project, the ELI wetlands program and economics staff have tried to summarize the lessons learned.

When ELI started this project we had a sense that it would lead us into many new and exciting lines of inquiry. It has done so, and we are not ready to quit. But it is now time to report on what we have learned to date in our work with Florida conservationists and with the Cary Trust.

As a national environmental research and publishing organization dedicated to the development of more effective and more efficient environmental protection and pollution control programs, the Environmental Law Institute is pleased to offer these findings. We hope the report will engender an intensified dialogue among scientists, economists, and lawyers on how to protect wetlands.

—J. William Futrell, President
Environmental Law Institute

# Chapter 1:
# Introduction

**W**etland loss and impairment are significant public policy concerns in the United States today. Recent advances in our understanding of ecological systems have made it clear that wetlands are important to society and that agricultural and water resource development have significantly diminished their quantity and quality. Both private and public development decisions have too often ignored the many goods and services generated by wetlands.

The federal government plays a role in many of the public and private projects that affect wetlands. Of the federal agencies involved in wetland development decisions, the U.S. Army Corps of Engineers probably plays the most important role. The Corps has primary responsibility for evaluating, constructing, and operating major water-related projects—such as dams, levees, canals, and dredging projects—associated with negative wetland impacts. The Corps is also charged with regulating development activities involving alteration or modification of navigable waters. The Corps thus assesses the desirability of many types of activities that have caused significant wetland loss in the United States. The federal Soil Conservation Service and Bureau of Reclamation also oversee activities with major impacts on wetlands. Lessons learned from studying the Corps can be readily applied to these other agencies, because their procedures are closely related to those of the Corps.

In deciding on the optimal mix of wetland development and preservation, federal agencies such as the Corps must balance the societal advantages and disadvantages of both. These advantages and disadvantages can best be evaluated if they can be incorporated into the economic framework of benefit-cost analysis. This framework requires development costs to be characterized in a form commensurable with that of development benefits. Development costs include wetland benefits foregone. In other words, wetland benefits diminished or eliminated by development must be expressed in dollars and cents, even though many of these benefits are not exchanged and priced in the marketplace. Modern techniques of natural resource and environmental economics make this expression possible for many types of wetland goods. Although far from perfect, these techniques have improved tremendously over the last 15 years. Given the necessary data, the state of the art now allows approximation of the dollar benefits of a wide range of natural resource characteristics and environmental goods, including nonmarket goods that in the past have been treated as "intangibles."

## The Corps' Current Benefit-Cost Framework and Its Flaws

In an effort to strike a balance between resource preservation and development, various statutes, regulations, and government policies establish benefit-cost frameworks designed to ensure that decisionmakers fully consider the social benefits of natural ecosystems as well as those of development. To achieve the right balance among alternative resource uses, a benefit-cost framework must be comprehensive, and decisionmakers must make full use of the available techniques for accurately expressing resource benefits in economic terms. However, economists and environmentalists have long recognized that the type of benefit-cost analysis conducted by the Corps and other federal water resource agencies in making wetland development decisions is defective on both counts. The framework is not comprehensive enough, and the agencies have rendered it even less useful by failing to take full advantage of current resource valuation capabilities.

Most importantly, agencies using the current framework have tended to ignore environmental costs lacking readily apparent market values. The agencies generally do not monetize such environmental impacts in their benefit-cost analyses, so they give these impacts less consideration than project benefits, which they do monetize. Failure to use economic valuation techniques to monetize and properly weigh environmental impacts leads decisionmakers to underestimate the true costs of development, and thus encourages wetland destruction.

It is admittedly difficult to incorporate the environmental costs of wetland development into federal benefit-cost analyses. Some of the reasons for this difficulty are economic, some are scientific, and some are political or institutional.

## Economic Problems

Easily applied wetland valuation methodologies are lacking. Standard economic techniques are not well-suited to valuing the effects of wetland development on human welfare. Since wetland goods are largely nonmarket goods, they must be carefully examined and valued using special techniques that can be complex and data-intensive. This is especially true of welfare changes resulting from wetland alteration. Moreover, economic valuation techniques, especially those related to nonmarket environmental goods, are difficult to integrate into existing administrative and regulatory processes. Although a tremendous amount of theoretical and empirical research has been conducted on economic valuation methods, relatively little attention has been paid to incorporating those methods into the administrative processes of wetland development decisionmaking.

## Scientific Problems

Valuation of welfare changes resulting from wetland alteration depends on detailed scientific information on how development might affect wetland goods and services. Despite recent advances in our knowledge of how wetlands contribute to human welfare, we still lack knowledge of how particular wetland characteristics interact to produce wetland goods and of how development affects these characteristics and thus the nature and supply of the resulting goods. Moreover, methodologies for quantifying wetland functions and their contributions to wetland outputs are not well developed, even for those functions about which scientific knowledge is greatest.

## Political/Institutional Problems

Nonmarket valuation techniques can best be applied in a decisionmaking process that is flexible enough to fit the needs of particular situations, yet specific enough to ensure correct application of the appropriate techniques. The current Corps process for making wetland development decisions does not fit this description, because it has been shaped by political and institutional forces that do not prioritize economically sound results. Most importantly, the governing benefit-cost criterion permits agencies such as the Corps to approve any project if its monetized benefits outweigh its monetized costs, without requiring them to make reasonable efforts to monetize—and thus to fully consider—environmental impacts. Because most wetland benefits that might be diminished or eliminated by development lack market values, benefit-cost analyses often do not monetize the costs of foregoing them. This is particularly troublesome because the federal agencies that conduct the benefit-cost analyses for water projects get the work if the projects are approved, and these analyses are inherently sensitive to the biases of those who conduct them.

## Themes of Monograph

This monograph explores the use of modern economics to improve wetland development decisionmaking, focusing on the barriers to adequate economic valuation of wetlands. Its fundamental conclusion is that most of these barriers are artifacts of scientific and political difficulties rather than limitations on economic methodologies. Existing economic techniques theoretically permit value estimation for many nonmarket wetland benefits, and for the changes in those benefits resulting from development. Estimation of these changes, however, requires extensive scientific input on the relationship of specific wetland characteristics to the provision of wetland goods, and on the effects of development on the characteristics and thus on the goods. Such detailed scientific knowledge is rarely available. In addition, economic techniques can be effective only if the relevant agencies are required to use them, and to use them properly. However, existing laws and regulations do not require use of the best available economic techniques for wetland valuation.

In the effort to allocate wetland resources efficiently, good economic methodology cannot overcome inadequate scientific understanding and biased political judgment. Because the three types of barriers to better wetlands valuation are synergistic, this monograph outlines the nature and interactions of all three and suggests ways to address them all. To improve the economics of the wetlands valuation process, we must first improve the science and politics of that process. It is perhaps especially important to improve the politics of wetland development decisionmaking in order to derive full benefit from ongoing advances in wetland science and nonmarket valuation.

The metaphor of technology-forcing helps explain how these problems interact and how their solutions may be integrated. Environmental problems have presented Congress with interwoven scientific, economic, and political issues before. In the case of air pollution, for example, Congress responded to this complex of problems by taking two steps. First, it required polluters to use available control mechanisms. Second, it set increasingly stringent future standards that could not be met using those mechanisms. The first step forced the use of existing pollution control technology; the second forced the development of new technology. This dual approach used political and legal coercion to advance the nation's ability to control air pollution. The problem of valuing wetlands may require a conceptually similar approach. Through an exercise of political will, Congress must force both the proper use of existing scientific and economic technology and the development of more sophisticated technology.

Another instructive analogy is the natural resource damages system established by federal hazardous waste law. Both wetland development and hazardous waste contamination of public natural resources have environmental as well as conventional economic effects that should be monetized to ensure economically efficient results. However, Congress has established different frameworks for the two problems. Examination of the natural resource damages framework helps clarify the flaws in the water resource development approach and suggests ways to improve that approach. The natural resource damages framework may be viewed as forcing the use and development of economic technology. At a minimum, it demonstrates that Congress is capable of changing the rules governing economic analysis of environmental problems and could, if it chose, change those rules to mandate proper economic valuation of wetlands.

## Organization of Monograph

Chapter Two of this monograph provides a working definition of wetlands and outlines the major causes of wetland loss in the United States. The chapter also describes the major wetland goods that contribute to human welfare, briefly reviews the ecological functions that produce those goods, and summarizes the limitations on scientific understanding that impede wetland valuation.

Chapter Three discusses the economic concepts underlying the valuation of nonmarket wetland goods, reviews the economic methodologies currently available for valuing wetlands, and outlines the existing barriers to broader application of those methodologies. Although this discussion is broadly applicable to wetland development decisionmaking, it is keyed to Corps decisionmaking and focuses particularly on the Corps' failure to consider the value of wetland goods lacking readily apparent dollar values. The review of valuation techniques has been simplified; the scope of this work does not permit a comprehensive review of the many relevant methodological questions and concerns. The discussion is intended to show a wider audience that existing economic methods, if properly applied, could lead to more complete accounting of the benefits and costs of wetland development. It is also intended to set the stage for more in-depth study of the use of economics in wetlands management.

Chapter Four discusses federal laws and guidelines on the use of economics in wetland development decisionmaking. It also reviews how federal agencies have implemented those laws and guidelines and summarizes the political and institutional barriers preventing the agencies from valuing wetlands properly. Like Chapter Three, it focuses on the Corps' decisionmaking, particularly the ways that the process accounts—or fails to account—for the environmental costs of development.

Chapter Five discusses the federal system for calculating natural resource damages. While not directly applicable to wetlands valuation, this system illustrates another potential approach to the use of economics in valuing environmental goods and thus may usefully be compared to the current wetlands valuation system.

Chapter Six recommends actions and research projects designed to encourage more thorough accounting of the environmental costs of federal water resource development. The recommendations include improvements in the scientific and economic assessment of wetland impacts, as well as institutional and administrative reforms designed to integrate nonmarket valuation methodologies into water project analyses.

# Chapter 2:
# The Science of Wetland Valuation

A s discussed in Chapter One, economic valuation of wetlands depends on, and is limited by, the state of the art in three fields: science, economics, and politics. This chapter focuses primarily on science. It first briefly defines wetlands and reviews the causes and magnitude of wetland destruction. It then describes the various wetland goods and services, or outputs, that contribute to human welfare and outlines what is known of the ecological functions that generate these outputs. The chapter concludes by summarizing the scientific difficulties underlying the wetland valuation problem and suggesting ways to conduct valuations in light of these difficulties.

**What Are Wetlands?**

Simply put, wetlands are lands that are periodically or seasonally wet. As such, they include both large and small ecosystems that go by various names, including bogs, potholes, swamps, and marshes. They occur when the water table is at or near the land surface or when the land is periodically covered by shallow water; they are thus characterized by soils that are inundated for at least part of the year and by various types of aquatic and semi-aquatic vegetation. Since they typically lie in depressions or along rivers, lakes, or coastal waters, they are subject to periodic flooding.

The Corps, EPA, the U.S. Fish and Wildlife Service (FWS), and the U.S. Soil Conservation Service define wetlands as lands having all three of the following attributes under ''normal circumstances'':

- at least periodically, the land supports aquatic vegetation;
- the substrate is predominantly undrained hydric soil (i.e., soil that is saturated or flooded long enough to produce the

anaerobic conditions that aquatic vegetation requires); and
* the substrate is saturated or covered by shallow water at some
time during the growing season of each year.[1]

The vast majority of U.S. wetlands fall into one of two broad
categories:

* estuarine (tidal or coastal) wetlands, which occur at the
boundary between dry land and saltwater; and
* freshwater (nontidal or inland) wetlands, which occur at the
boundary between dry land and freshwater. More than 90 percent of U.S. wetlands are freshwater wetlands.[2]

## Wetland Loss: Causes and Trends

Wetlands have been drained, filled, and otherwise altered for various
types of development to such an extent that less than half of the original
wetland acreage in the lower 48 states remains today. The FWS has
estimated that of the 215 million wetland acres believed to have ex-
isted when European settlement began, only 99 million acres remained
by the mid-1970s.

FWS data indicate that from the mid-1950s to 1974, the United
States lost approximately 9 million acres of wetlands, or approximately
450,000 acres per year.[3] Agricultural development was estimated to
be responsible for about 87 percent of these losses, urban development for 8 percent, and other activities for the remaining 5 percent.[4]

It has been estimated that 91 million wetland acres remained in
the lower 48 states as of 1982, which indicates a loss of approximately
8 million acres between 1974 and 1982, or 1 million acres per year.[5]
This is more than double the loss rate from the 1950s to the 1970s.
A surge of agricultural development was probably the primary reason
for the increase. Relatively high agricultural prices as well as a strong
agricultural export market during this period probably made agricultural conversion of wetlands more profitable.

It is widely believed that wetland losses have slowed considerably
since the early 1980s. Losses in the mid-1980s are estimated at 200,000
to 400,000 acres per year. The decreased loss rate is probably due to
various federal and state protection measures and, most importantly,
to a general decline in the rate at which wetlands were drained for
agriculture. The available evidence suggests that implementation of
the Federal Water Pollution Control Act (FWPCA) §404 permit program in the late 1970s and of state protection measures inspired by

the Coastal Zone Management Act of 1972 have inhibited coastal wetland losses. Inland wetland losses appear to have decreased primarily as a result of a large decline in new agricultural drainage, although little hard facts are available. Agricultural drainage is probably still the major cause of continuing losses of inland wetlands. Water projects, flood control measures, navigation, water supply projects, and residential and commercial development contribute to continuing losses of both inland and coastal wetlands.

## Wetland Outputs

Table 2.1 lists some of the major outputs of wetland ecosystems. These outputs are divided into three major classes based on the ways that they ultimately benefit society. Although some outputs fall into more than one class, the division remains useful, because the different classes generally require different valuation approaches.

### Intermediate Wetland Goods

The first class of wetland outputs consists of intermediate goods, which serve as factors of production for other goods. This class includes commercial and damage prevention factors. Commercial factors are those that contribute to production of final commercial goods. That is, they are combined with other factors, such as labor and capital, to produce final goods sold in commercial markets. Perhaps the most economically important commercial goods that rely on wetland factors of production are fisheries products. Coastal estuaries and their wetlands help to produce commercially important fish and shellfish by providing food and spawning and nursery grounds. Wetlands also support and provide habitat for other commercially harvested flora and fauna, such as timber and small fur-bearing mammals. Wetland groundwater recharge and water storage are important factors in production of water for drinking or for agricultural irrigation. Finally, wetland abilities to store and remove nutrients have been factors in advanced treatment of human wastes.

    While commercial factors are linked primarily to the production of specific market goods, damage prevention factors contribute to a wider range of activities. These environmental services typically reduce natural and human-induced damage to property and natural resources, thereby lowering the cost of producing a wide variety of commercial and noncommercial outputs. For example, wetlands often control

### Table 2.1
### Wetland Outputs

I. Intermediate Goods and Services (serve as factors of production for other goods)

    A.   Commercial factors (serve as factors of production for market goods)
- Support of commercial fisheries
- Provision of commercially harvested natural resources (e.g., timber, peat, small fur-bearing mammals)
- Water supply and storage
- Assimilation of wastes (e.g., for tertiary treatment of human wastes)

    B.   Damage prevention factors (serve as factors of production for a wide variety of goods and services)
- Pollution assimilation/water purification
- Flood control
- Erosion prevention

II. Final Goods and Services (produce consumer satisfaction directly)

    A.   Recreational opportunities
- Consumptive uses (e.g., fishing and hunting)
- Nonconsumptive uses (e.g., camping, hiking, boating, birdwatching)

    B.   Amenities
- Scenic value
- Spiritual value
- Education

III. Future Goods and Services (may fall into any of the categories above)

    A.   Undiscovered goods

    B.   Future high-value development

flooding in adjacent and down-gradient communities, thus reducing the cost of flood control measures. In addition, by taking up and removing or immobilizing nutrients, heavy metals, and toxic substances, wetlands effectively reduce water pollution caused by non-point-source runoff. This water purification function reduces the cost of treating surface waters used for domestic water supplies and helps prevent eutrophication, which is detrimental to aquatic wildlife used for commercial and recreational purposes.

*Final Wetland Goods*

The second major class of wetland outputs consists of final goods, which are consumed to satisfy human wants directly. This class includes recreational goods and amenities. Recreational goods provided by wetlands include opportunities for hiking, camping, birdwatching, and nature study. They also include activities (e.g., fishing and hunting) that rely on wildlife which uses wetland habitats either permanently or seasonally. Amenities provided by wetlands include the scenic value of their open spaces and flora and fauna to the general public, especially to adjacent communities. Amenities also include any spiritual value that individuals might associate with the knowledge that such natural areas exist.

*Future Wetland Goods*

Within each of these two major classes of wetland outputs is an important sub-class of future goods and services. For example, a gene pool associated with wetland flora and fauna may lead to future discoveries of new goods, such as medicines.

**Ecological Functions of Wetlands**

It is the ecological functions of wetlands that generate wetland goods. Some of these functions have only recently been fully recognized; the last two decades have seen the development of a substantial body of scientific literature in this area. Existing scientific knowledge is generally sufficient to identify the wetland characteristics that are indicators of particular wetland goods. However, despite this progress in understanding wetland functions, we still need to learn much more about their underlying characteristics before we can measure them on a large scale. Methodologies for quantifying wetland functions and their contributions to the production of goods and services are not well-developed even for those functions on which scientific knowledge is greatest.

The major ecological functions of wetland ecosystems are briefly summarized below in terms of the current levels of scientific understanding of these functions, the important factors and processes that determine their existence and significance, the types of wetlands with which they are most often associated, and their current amenability to measurement.[6]

## Flood Storage and Desynchronization

Flood storage and desynchronization is the process by which wetland basins store and gradually release peak water flows from precipitation or upland runoff. Wetlands that perform this function may provide significant flood control services to nearby communities.

It is generally agreed that wetlands associated with streams may control and desynchronize floods. Freshwater wetlands associated with upper parts of river systems may perform this function particularly well. Coastal wetlands also store flood waters, thus reducing the flood impact of major storms.[7] Factors that may affect the flood control function include the following:

- storm magnitude and duration;
- ability of upslope area to retain and dissipate runoff;
- above-ground basin storage capacity;
- below-ground basin storage capacity; and
- position of wetland basin in watershed.

We presently lack the techniques and information necessary to assess the exact nature of wetland flood control or to measure the flood control effectiveness of particular wetlands or wetland types.[8]

## Groundwater Recharge and Discharge

Groundwater recharge is the downward movement of surface waters and precipitation into groundwater systems; groundwater discharge is the upward or lateral movement of subsurface waters into surface waters. Recharge may replenish nearby domestic, agricultural, and industrial water supplies, while discharge may be critical for maintaining soil moisture in adjacent agricultural areas.

While some wetlands appear to recharge aquifer systems, most do not. Temporary or seasonal wetlands seem more likely to do so than permanent wetlands.[9] More wetlands appear to perform groundwater discharge. The following factors affect wetland groundwater functions:

- direction (into or out of the aquifer) and location (within the basin) of groundwater movement;
- groundwater flow rates and storage capacity; and
- evapotranspiration rates.

We have limited information on the potential groundwater recharge and discharge functions of wetlands. Recharge, for example, has been studied less than any other wetland function, so the role wetlands may play in recharging aquifers is poorly understood. Much more work is needed before we can adequately measure the interaction between wetlands and groundwater functions.

### Shoreline Anchoring and Dissipation of Erosive Forces

Shoreline anchoring is the process by which the root systems of wetland vegetation stabilize soil at the water's edge and enhance the accretion of soil and/or peat at the shoreline. Dissipation of erosive forces is the process by which wetland vegetation diminishes the erosive impact on soil of waves, currents, and general water level fluctuations. Wetlands are thought to play significant roles in anchoring soil and controlling erosion. These wetland functions protect both natural resources and man-made structures by inhibiting shoreline erosion and the creation of eroded sediments that can cause siltation of navigable waterways.

Larger wetlands with extensive, persistent vegetation (e.g., forested wetlands) are probably the most effective at dissipating erosive forces. For example, studies suggest that vegetated freshwater wetland basins and coastal and fringe cypress wetlands are relatively effective at shoreline anchoring. Other wetlands, such as prairie potholes, play a far less significant role. The following factors affect these wetland functions:

- energy of erosive forces;
- frictional resistance of wetland;
- type of wetland vegetation and ability of root systems to anchor soil;

- erodibility of adjacent fastland; and
- position of wetland relative to fastland and incoming erosive forces.

We currently have inadequate evidence on the exact contribution of most types of wetlands to shoreline anchoring and erosion control. More research is needed on the types of wetland plant communities that may perform these functions.[10]

*Nutrient Retention and Removal*

Nutrient retention is the process by which wetlands store nutrient wastes, such as phosphorus and nitrogen, within their soils and vegetation. Nutrient removal is the process by which wetlands release these retained wastes. Denitrification, for example, converts retained nitrogen wastes to gas and releases them from the wetland system. These wetland functions may keep pollutants in urban and agricultural runoff from reaching ground and surface waters, thereby preventing contamination of potable water supplies and protecting commercial and recreational fisheries by controlling eutrophication. Wetland nutrient retention and removal capabilities are in some cases utilized for tertiary treatment of human wastes.

It is believed that all wetlands serve as nutrient traps to varying degrees. Wetlands generally retain nutrients more effectively than uplands do, and most wetlands, particularly those with fine, anoxic sediments, also store and remove nutrients. Anoxic soils retard decomposition, thus promoting long-term nutrient storage within bottom sediments. These soils also promote denitrification, which decreases the release of nutrients into water flow. Studies indicate that freshwater wetlands are most efficient at removing nutrients. A wetland's efficiency in retaining and removing nutrients depends on many characteristics, including type of vegetation, nature of substrate, size, water chemistry, temperature, and pH. The following factors have been identified as characteristic of wetland ecosystems performing valuable nutrient retention and removal functions.

- The wetland vegetation assimilates and transfers to deep sediment more nutrients than are subsequently released by leaching and decay, and it does so most efficiently when downstream waters are most vulnerable to nutrient enrichment.
- The substrate accumulates more organic matter than is released into water systems through decomposition.

• Sediments accumulate faster than they are removed, and the nutrients contained in these sediments remain intact.
• The rate of denitrification exceeds that of nitrogen fixation.

More study is necessary to determine the exact role that wetlands play in improving water quality. For example, no literature suggests general criteria for measuring levels of wetland nutrient retention.

## Aquatic Food Chain Support

The aquatic food chain support function refers to the direct and indirect use of wetland-derived nutrients by fish and shellfish. This function is known to be important to the production of commercial and sport estuarine fish and shellfish.

Wetlands are typically more effective producers and exporters of useful nutrients than terrestrial systems. The extent to which a wetland performs these functions depends primarily on its net primary productivity (NPP) and nutrient export. NPP is the degree to which wetland plants convert solar energy to carbon, gaseous nitrogen to nitrate, and inorganic nutrients to useful organic compounds. Nutrient export is the movement of these nutrient food sources out of the wetland and into surface waters. Of the two, nutrient export is believed to be potentially more important. Adamus and Stockwell state that a wetland's effectiveness at nutrient export and food chain support depends on affirmative answers to the following questions.

• Are the annual NPP and nitrogen-fixing ability of the wetland, per unit area, as high as or higher than those of adjacent terrestrial (e.g., riparian leaf fall) or independent deep water (e.g., planktonic) communities?
• Is the detritus that represents this productivity flushed out of the wetland at an appropriate time and transported to areas where fish and aquatic invertebrates can consume it directly or indirectly, or can it be consumed by organisms present near the point where it is produced?
• Do fish and invertebrates really use and prefer the wetland plant detritus and/or its decomposition products as a direct or indirect food source?
• Is food the primary factor limiting fish or invertebrate productivity, or are space, water quality, harvest regulations, or other factors more significant?

The aquatic food chain support function is quite complex, and we lack information on the processes underlying it. More study of the breakdown and movement of nutrients through aquatic food chains is needed before this function can be properly evaluated and its significance determined.[11]

*Fisheries Habitat Support*

The fisheries habitat support function refers to the "physical and chemical factors which affect the metabolism, attachment, and predator avoidance of the adult or larval forms."[12] This function is widely recognized as important; wetlands provide both nursery grounds and food for many species of freshwater and saltwater fish. Most commercial saltwater fish and shellfish depend on coastal estuaries and their wetlands for spawning grounds and nurseries. The contribution of wetlands to fish production is well established for the Atlantic, Gulf, and Northern Pacific coastal areas. Fish found in freshwater wetlands usually depend on the forage those wetlands provide. Moreover, many of the larger freshwater fish enter wetlands to feed or spawn, generally on a daily or seasonal basis. The nursery function of wetlands for large game fish is well documented for Great Lakes wetlands, but less so for other freshwater wetlands.

The following factors are important to this wetland function:

- water quality (physical and chemical);
- water quantity (hydroperiod, flow, and depth); and
- cover, substrate, and interspersion.

Salinity and temperature are very important to the water quality of marine and estuarine fisheries; dissolved oxygen and turbidity are occasionally important. Temperature and dissolved oxygen are important to the water quality of freshwater wetlands; turbidity, salinity, and pH are sometimes important. Depth, volume, velocity, width, and hydroperiod are all important factors affecting water quantity.

*Wildlife Habitat Support*

Wildlife habitat support is the provision of environmental features that supply the food and shelter needs of birds, mammals, and other wildlife. This function gives people the opportunity to engage in bird-watching, hunting, and other wildlife-oriented recreational activities.

In many regions, species diversity and wildlife population densities in wetlands are sometimes lower than those in adjacent uplands. However, wetlands contribute to the presence of many species that would otherwise be absent from the regional fauna. The wetland dependence of a given species may vary greatly with the abundance and distribution of wetlands and suitable alternative habitats within a region. While only a few species of mammals are totally wetland-dependent, individual populations of many species are wetland-dependent in some areas at certain times of the year. Totally wetland-dependent species include muskrats, beavers, marsh rice rats, and swamp rabbits. Partially wetland-dependent species include mink, raccoon, meadow mice, moose, and white-tailed deer.

Factors affecting a wetland's wildlife support function include the following:

- availability of cover and freedom from disturbance;
- availability of food; and
- availability of specialized habitat needs.

Specific wetland habitat requirements are best known for some animals of economic importance, such as fish, shellfish, waterfowl, and fur-bearing animals. Relatively little is known about the wetland habitat requirements of other mammals and birds.

## Scientific Barriers to Economic Valuation of Wetlands

As the previous discussion suggests, recent advances in wetland science have greatly increased our understanding of the many ways in which wetlands contribute to human welfare. By observing the biological and physical characteristics of wetland systems, we can generally identify the presence or absence of wetland functions that give rise to specific wetland goods. By identifying those functions for regional wetland systems, we can then generally pinpoint which goods and services the systems produce. This is a substantially higher level of understanding than was possible 20 years ago.

Despite our increased knowledge, models for empirically estimating the linkages among wetland characteristics, functions, and benefits are still in the early stages of development. Our ability to quantify the relationships between wetland characteristics and functions is limited. It is perhaps more troublesome that even when we have data on the functions of a specific wetland system, we cannot quantitatively estimate the quality and quantity of goods and services that it produces. Yet these linkages must be estimated for regional wetland systems before economic methodologies can be used to estimate how development of those systems might change human welfare.

These scientific limitations, however, should not preclude attempts to estimate wetland values for purposes of public decisionmaking. As water resource development continues to threaten wetland quality and quantity, we must continue to try to ascertain the magnitude of the wetland values at risk. Until we develop comprehensive regional wetland models capable of empirically estimating the links between observed (predevelopment) and predicted (postdevelopment) wetland characteristics, functions, and goods and services, wetland valuation efforts must proceed based on what we do know. In a world of incomplete information, we must do the best we can.

Specifically, we should use existing wetland assessment methodologies to identify the most important functions of regional wetland systems. The values of the wetland goods and services believed to be derived from those functions can then be assessed and aggregated based on observations of wetland use levels. For example, if wetland functional assessments indicate that a particular coastal wetland system provides vital nursery and feeding grounds for a nearby shellfishery, the wetland's contribution to the shellfishery can be estimated based on observed shellfish harvests. While this approach does not indicate how wetland alteration might change wetland values, it does indicate the potential magnitude of the values at risk.

## Notes to Chapter 2

1. *See* Federal Water Pollution Control Act (FWPCA) §404, 33 U.S.C. §1344, ELR STAT. FWPCA 054; 33 C.F.R. §323.2(c); U.S. FISH AND WILDLIFE SERVICE, U.S. DEP'T OF THE INTERIOR, CLASSIFICATION OF WETLANDS AND DEEPWATER HABITATS OF THE UNITED STATES, REPORT NO. FWS/OBS-79-31 (1979). A joint FEDERAL MANUAL FOR IDENTIFYING AND DELINEATING WETLANDS, issued in January 1989, eliminated previous differences among federal agencies' definitions of wetlands.

2. The minority of wetlands that are not in one of these categories are hybrids of the two.

3. These numbers were derived by comparing FWS surveys done in the mid-1950s and in 1974. Over the last few decades the FWS has tracked U.S. wetland loss using aerial photography and ground mapping.

4. R. TINER, WETLANDS OF THE UNITED STATES: CURRENT STATUS AND RECENT TRENDS (U.S. Fish and Wildlife Service, U.S. Dep't of Interior, 1984).

5. R. HEIMLICH & L. LANGNER, SWAMPBUSTING: WETLAND CONVERSION AND FARM PROGRAMS (Economic Research Service, U.S. Dep't of Agriculture, Report No. 551, 1986). This estimate was based on the most recent comprehensive wetland inventory, which was conducted by the U.S. Soil Conservation Service as part of its 1982 National Resources Inventory, together with supplemental data.

6. These summaries draw chiefly from two reviews of the scientific literature performed by the FWS. *See* 1 P. ADAMUS & L. STOCKWELL, A METHOD FOR WETLAND FUNCTIONAL ASSESSMENT: CRITICAL REVIEW AND EVALUATION CONCEPTS (Report No. FHWA-IP-82-23, Federal Highway Administration, U.S. Dep't of Transportation, 1983); J. SATHER & R. SMITH, AN OVERVIEW OF MAJOR WETLAND FUNCTIONS AND VALUES (Report No. FWS/OBS-84/18, 1984) (performed for Western Energy and Land Use Team, U.S. Fish and Wildlife Service, U.S. Dep't of Interior).

7. FISH AND WILDLIFE SERVICE, U.S. DEP'T OF INTERIOR, DRAFT REPORT TO CONGRESS: COASTAL BARRIERS RESOURCES SYSTEM EXECUTIVE SUMMARY (1987).

8. Studies on this wetland function have generally been restricted to glacial areas. *See, e.g.,* J. LARSON, MODELS FOR EVALUATION OF FRESHWATER WETLANDS (Report No. 32, University of Massachusetts, Amherst, 1976); NEW ENGLAND DIVISION, U.S. ARMY CORPS OF ENGINEERS, CHARLES RIVER MAIN REPORT AND ATTACHMENT (1972).

9. Studies in Massachusetts have concluded that wetlands in this glacial region have significant recharge functions.

10. Investigations of these functions have generally been plant-specific rather

than covering entire wetland plant communities. While the roots of all wetland plants can bind soil, it is unclear whether this process is significant enough to protect entire shorelines.

11. The strongest evidence for the aquatic food chain support function has been found in estuaries in the southeastern Gulf states. However, some studies have questioned this link. Recent studies of Atlantic and Pacific coastal marshes offer no conclusive evidence.

12. P. ADAMUS & L. STOCKWELL, *supra* note 7.

# Chapter 3:
# Principles and Methods for Valuing Wetland Goods

---

I n deciding whether to alter a particular wetland for water resource purposes, the federal government tries to balance the societal benefits and costs of the alteration. This approach places a premium on accurately assessing wetland value, especially the changes in value expected to result from development. This chapter focuses on the economics of assessing wetland value. It first explains why the marketplace does not accurately reflect wetland values and describes the economic basis for valuing nonmarket goods. It then outlines the major steps in valuing wetland outputs generally, reviews the various economic techniques available for valuing particular types of non-market wetland outputs, summarizes the difficulties in using these techniques, and suggests ways to proceed in the face of these difficulties.

**Inability of the Market System to Allocate Wetlands Efficiently**

If, as discussed in Chapter Two, wetlands provide such valuable benefits to society, why are they so frequently converted to agricultural or urban uses? One reason is that the market assigns wetlands a relatively low price. This is due largely to the nature of the benefits and beneficiaries of wetlands and of development.

Many wetland outputs are what economists call "positive undepletable externalities," more commonly referred to as "public goods," that exist outside immediate wetland areas. Examples discussed in Chapter Two include flood control and pollution reduction. These goods are non-rival in consumption and thus are not exclusive. In other words, an increase in one person's consumption of such a good does not preclude or reduce its availability to others. This characteristic of wetland outputs, coupled with the extension of many of these outputs beyond immediate wetland areas, prevents wetland owners from charging fees for the benefits they provide to society. For example, if a privately owned wetland controls flooding in adjacent communities, the owner cannot charge community members for this service because he cannot withhold it from those who do not pay.

Since wetland owners cannot recoup the value of the benefits that wetlands provide to society, the marketplace price per acre does not fully reflect the true exchange value of wetlands relative to other goods and services. As a result, many owners find it most profitable to convert wetlands to agricultural use or sell them to developers.[1]

### Definition of "Economic Value"

The economic benefit to society of any good or service is defined as the dollar amount that the public is willing to pay for the good or service rather than be without it. This measure of welfare is formally expressed in a concept called willingness to pay (WTP). The WTP definition of welfare derives from the wants and preferences of present generations based on their wealth and knowledge of available goods and services. Importantly, it assumes that preferences can be expressed in monetary terms. In other words, it assumes that an individual can translate a reduction in some good, such as a wetland good, into the dollar amount (net WTP) that would compensate the individual for this loss. In aggregate, the net WTP measure of wetland benefits represents the monetary value that society places on wetland goods.

The most direct and visible monetary symbol for a good is its market price, and considerable confusion exists among noneconomists concerning the relationship between a good's market price and its value in terms of WTP. On first reflection, one might conclude that if an individual buys a certain good at its market price of $10, $10 is what the individual is willing to pay for this particular good, and thus is its value to the individual. However, this is not necessarily true. If an individual spends $10 to obtain a good, we know only that the good is worth at least this much to the individual. The individual may also have been willing to spend more, for example $12, to obtain the good. In this case, the $10 market price is only a lower bound estimate of the *total value* of the good to the individual, that is, the individual's total WTP for the good.

Based on this discussion, one might erroneously conclude that total market expenditures for a good (i.e., price times quantity sold) would constitute a lower bound estimate of its consumer value. The problem with this conclusion is that the appropriate economic measure of welfare or value is *net benefits*, not total value. The net benefits society derives from a good are represented by *net WTP*, or the amount society would be willing to pay to produce and/or use a good *beyond* that which it actually does pay.

To illustrate the concept of economic value based on net WTP, consider the case in which only one unit of a certain good is produced at a cost of $7 and sold at a price of $10. If the purchaser had been willing to pay $12, the net benefit of the good to this consumer is $2 ($12 less $10). Moreover, the producer earns $3 from the sale, so the net benefit of the good to the producer is $3. The total economic value of the good is thus $5 ($2 net benefit to the consumer plus $3 net benefit to the producer). If for some reason the producer was denied the opportunity to produce and sell—and the consumer the opportunity to buy and use—the good, the total loss to these individuals would be $5.

The same principle holds for goods that do not have observable market prices. For example, consider the case of a fisherman who would be willing to spend up to $30 a day to use a particular fishing site, but only has to spend $20 a day in travel and associated costs. The net benefit or economic value to the fisherman of a fishing day at the site is not the $20 expenditure, but the $10 difference between what he would be willing to spend and what he actually has to spend. If a development project eliminated all fishing opportunity at the site, the fisherman would lose the satisfaction of fishing there, as represented by $10 a day in net benefits. The $20 a day he would have spent to visit the site would not be lost but would be available for him to spend elsewhere.

Because market expenditures do not directly convey any information about net benefits, we cannot use expenditures on a particular good or on related goods purchased in conjunction with it as a direct measure of the social value of the good. Furthermore, when a structural change in the cost of producing a good results in a change in its price, the ensuing change in expenditures for the good does not directly say anything about the change in its economic value to users.

Although markets do not directly indicate the economic values of goods, this does not mean they are not useful for estimating those values. On the contrary, because a market provides a forum for society to express relative preferences in monetary terms, market transactions can be used to infer preferences, and thus economic values. Also, nonmarket goods can sometimes be valued based on information on preferences provided by market transactions for related products.

In attempting to measure the aggregate satisfaction that society as a whole derives from a good or service, economists often use the concepts of consumer surplus and economic rent to approximate net WTP. When a good is exchanged in a perfectly competitive market, its market price, which is determined by the equilibrium of demand (i.e., marginal WTP) and supply (i.e., marginal cost), measures consumers' marginal WTP for the last unit of the good purchased. For all other units of the good purchased, however, consumers' marginal WTP for each unit exceeds market price. The excess of what consumers are willing to pay over what they actually do pay for the total quantity of a good purchased is called consumer surplus. This represents the use value of the good to consumers in terms of net WTP, and is represented by the area under the good's demand curve, bounded by price. Moreover, a good's market-clearing price also corresponds to the marginal cost of producing the last unit of output. For all other units of the good produced, however, producers' marginal production cost for each unit is less than market price. The excess of what producers earn over their production costs for the total quantity of a good sold is called producer surplus or economic rent. This represents the production value or net benefit of the good to producers, and it is represented by the area over the good's supply curve, bounded by price. While not an exact measure of social welfare, the sum of consumer surplus and economic rent provides a useful approximation of the net benefit of a good or service.

For goods traded in the marketplace, observable price and quantity data provide the basis for estimating demand, and prices of production inputs and knowledge of production relationships provide the basis for estimating supply. For most market goods, it is relatively straightforward (although not easy) to empirically estimate the relevant demand and supply relationships and use these to estimate net benefits, as well as changes in net benefits resulting from structural changes in either demand or supply.

Estimating the net benefits of goods that generally are not exchanged in the marketplace, such as most goods provided by wetlands, is much more difficult. Because these goods do not have observable market prices, economists search for unobserved (implicit) prices that may be used to construct the relevant demand and supply relationships. These implicit prices may be sought through indirect or direct means. The indirect, or "revealed preference," approach links the use of a nonmarket good to some closely related market choice. Valuation methodologies using this approach include the factor income, travel cost, and hedonic pricing techniques. In contrast, the direct approach attempts to elicit preferences for nonmarket goods by asking individuals to express their views in a simulated market for those goods. Contingent valuation methodologies use this approach.

These direct and indirect valuation methodologies may be used to approximate the economic value of nonmarket wetland goods. For final wetland outputs that produce no economic rent (e.g., recreational opportunities), one need only estimate consumers' net WTP for their use. For intermediate wetland goods that serve as inputs into the production of market goods (e.g., support of commercial fisheries), the analysis conversely focuses on the economic rent accruing to producers of the market good after payments to all other production inputs.[2]

## General Framework for Valuation of Wetlands Before and After Alteration

The discussion to this point has focused primarily on estimation of existing net benefits, such as those provided by wetlands before they are modified by water resource development. Such valuations can be performed with limited knowledge regarding the link between wetland ecological functions and wetland goods. They only require sufficient evidence that particular wetlands produce or support the goods to be valued, and that elimination of the wetlands would eliminate or severely diminish the quantity and/or quality of those goods. Given such evidence, together with information regarding public use of the goods, nonmarket valuation techniques can be directly applied to estimating the net benefits provided by those goods.

However, efficient water resource planning requires knowledge not only of the predevelopment values of wetland ecosystems, but also of their postdevelopment values. Ideally, it requires prediction of the degree to which a water project will change wetland benefits. This prediction is much more difficult than simple inference of pre-development net benefits based on observation of consumers' and producers' use of wetland goods. To estimate changes in the net benefits provided by wetland goods, valuation techniques must be keyed to specific changes in the nature and supply of those goods. Estimation of changes in net benefits thus requires far more detailed information on the link between wetland characteristics and wetland goods than does estimation of predevelopment benefits.

Measurement of the economic benefit derived from a particular wetland good or service and of that benefit's potential response to wetland alteration generally involves three steps. First, the analyst must identify the good and how the wetland produces it. This requires identifying and estimating the level of the wetland functions that give rise to the good, and estimating how those functions relate to the ecological characteristics that the proposed project may affect. Next, the analyst must determine the nature and supply of the good. This involves estimating how various wetland characteristics relate to that nature and supply—for example, how a wetland's various habitat attributes relate to the type and number of game animals supported.[3] Finally, the analyst must determine the use and economic value of the good and how these relate to its nature and supply. For a final wetland good, for example, this requires estimating the demand for the good and how this demand relates to some measure of its nature and supply.

A proposed alteration of wetland attributes would affect the quantity and quality of a wetland good, in turn affecting how consumers and producers use that good. This change in user behavior would change the benefit provided by the good. Given knowledge of the physical and economic relationships linking wetland ecological characteristics to the final use of a wetland good, the three steps above could be used to estimate both the economic benefit originally provided by the good and the way that wetland alteration might affect this benefit.

Comprehensive economic valuation of present and future wetland goods ideally requires modeling and estimation of the physical and economic relationships underlying wetland goods production and use in an entire systems context.[4] Systems analysis in the wetlands valuation context is a kind of input-output model containing the interrelated set of functional relationships between wetland ecological characteristics and processes and production and utilization of wetland goods. Development of such a model for a regional wetland ecosystem would permit prediction of changes in wetland benefits resulting from proposed wetland alterations. The ideal model would be a holistic one, capable of estimating the benefits of all the goods and services provided by a particular wetland tract or region and the potential changes in these benefits resulting from site alteration.

Unfortunately, such a model will be difficult, if not impossible, to develop. It demands knowledge of the physical and economic relationships underlying all wetland goods, and this knowledge is currently lacking in several respects. First, we have limited understanding of wetland functions and limited ability to measure and quantify those functions. Moreover, even given adequate knowledge of the wetland attributes describing specific functions, identification of how these attributes contribute to the quantity and quality of wetland service flows is problematic. Very little work has been reported on the measurement of physical linkages that explain and predict the nature and supply of wetland goods, especially ecological goods and services; most of the work to date has dealt only with the relationships of wildlife habitat attributes' to wildlife population measures. Also, identification and measurement of the economic linkages relating consumer behavior to the nature of service flows are advancing for recreational goods and services, but not for ecological goods and services.

Given the unavailability of regional models for evaluating the effects of development on wetland benefits, economists must take a second-best approach to wetlands valuation. This involves identifying as many of the goods and services associated with a particular wetland ecosystem as available information allows and applying economic techniques to value their *current uses*. While this approach does not yield an estimate of the change in wetland values associated with wetland alteration, it does yield an estimate of the magnitude of wetland benefits at risk. The remainder of this chapter discusses the various techniques available for wetland valuation primarily in this context and briefly outlines the minimum data and methodological requirements that would permit estimation of value changes associated with wetland modification.

## Economic Techniques for Valuing Nonmarket Outputs

The following discussion briefly reviews the WTP-based methodologies that could be used to determine the economic value of different types of nonmarket wetland goods. The discussion also examines certain valuation methodologies that are not based on economic concepts, but that might be used under certain conditions to obtain surrogate estimates of use value. The valuation methods are grouped according to the types of wetland goods to which they are most applicable. Table 3.1 matches valuation techniques with types of wetland outputs.[5]

*Valuation of Intermediate Wetland Goods: Commercial Inputs*

As discussed in Chapter Two, commercial wetland inputs are wetland goods that contribute to the production of commercial goods such as fish and shellfish products, domestic water supplies, agricultural

## Table 3.1.
## Valuation Approaches By Wetland Goods

| Method | Commercial Factors | Damage Prevention Factors | | | | | Final Wetland Goods | | |
|---|---|---|---|---|---|---|---|---|---|
|  | All | Water Supply | Flood Control | Storm Protection | Tertiary Waste Treatment | Erosion Control | Recreation | Amenities | Nonuse Benefit |
| Net Factor Income | X | X | | | X | | | | |
| Travel Cost | | | | | | | X | | |
| Contingent Valuation | | | | | | | X | X | X |
| Property Value | | | | | | | | X | |
| Replacement Cost | | X | | | X | | | | |
| Damage Cost | | | X | X | | X | | | |

products, pelts of small animals, peat, and timber. As factors of production, wetland goods contribute to the economic profits in these markets. However, the price paid (if any) for use of a wetland good typically does not reflect its true economic value to producers. A more accurate measure of the economic value of such a good is the amount that producers would be willing to pay for its use as a fixed factor of production, above what they actually do pay. This is the economic rent attributable to use of the wetland good in production. The methodology discussed below may be used to approximate this measure of economic value. It may also be used to approximate the change in economic value resulting from a wetland modification if the price of the market good and the prices of all nonwetland production inputs can be assumed to remain the same.

☐ *Net Factor Income (NFI) Method.* As its name implies, the NFI method measures the appropriate income to natural resources as factors of production in commercial activities. The method estimates the economic profits of commercial activities after payments are made to all other factors of production (including labor, capital, and management). These profits correspond to the value of the natural resources in commercial production.

The NFI methodology relies on an understanding of the production process for the market good and ideally would involve development of a formal model of this process. Such a model would relate the variable production inputs, including the wetland good, to production of the market good. For example, the contribution of groundwater to the production of domestic water supply could be valued using an economic/engineering model of that production.

Some applications of the NFI method have attempted such formal modeling of the relevant physical production and economic linkages. For example, attempts to estimate the value of wetlands in production of blue crabs on the Florida Gulf Coast[6] and oysters in Virginia[7] used bioeconomic modeling to relate wetland services to the production of specific commercial goods. The marginal physical contributions of wetlands to production of the market goods were derived from these production relationships and were used to approximate the net social benefit provided by the intermediate wetland services.

When there is no such formal model, however, as is often the case, the NFI method can be applied given knowledge of the market good's production costs and sales revenue. To illustrate this simplified

NFI method, consider the problem of valuing the contribution of a wetland-supported estuary to a commercial fishery.[8] Here, the NFI method calculates economic profits to fishermen as a proxy for the value attributable to use of the estuary as an input into fish production. Total revenue received by fishermen for the estuary-dependent fish species landed in a region is used as an estimate of the gross value of the fishery. To estimate the profits attributable to wetlands, the total cost of capturing the fish (payments to all factors of production, including appropriate payments to fishermen as managers) is subtracted from total gross value. The result is an estimate of economic profit that measures producers' net WTP for use of the wetlands-supported estuary as a fixed factor in commercial production.

The simplified NFI approach is an appealing technique for valuing wetland support of commercial activities because its methodology is straightforward and its data requirements limited. It does not require much information on the actual physical contribution of wetland outputs to commercial activities. In the fishery case, for example, it ignores the linkages among wetlands, fish biomass, and fish production.

Use of the NFI method to measure the value changes that will result from proposed wetland alterations is more data-intensive. It requires knowledge of the physical and economic relationships linking wetland characteristics to yields of all the commercial goods to which those characteristics contribute. When the ecological production relationships are not well known (as in the case of wetland support of commercial fisheries), they must be assumed on the basis that the wetland is known to contribute something to production of the final good. For other types of intermediate wetland services (e.g., support of fur trapping, irrigation water supply), these relationships may be better known, and the data required to quantify them more readily available. For these services, it may be possible to predict the decrease in the commercial yields, total revenue, and net profit that would result from a given wetland alteration, and thus the change in the wetland's contribution to the commercial activity.

The general NFI approach to measuring changes in value involves incorporating available information on the physical production and economic linkages between wetland acreage and a commercial activity into an equation relating production of the good to its factors of production (labor, capital, and wetlands). Statistical estimation of this type of production relationship yields parameter estimates that represent the marginal physical contribution of each production input, including wetlands. Marginal physical contribution represents the contribution to production of the last unit of the input employed. This measure multiplied by the product price corresponds to the value of that last unit.

The study by Lynne and colleagues provides a good illustration of this general methodology. The study used models of fish population dynamics, including crab growth and mortality, to develop a proxy variable for wetlands contribution to crab biomass. This was included as an independent variable in an equation relating annual harvest to levels of factors of production. Estimation of this production function using data over time yielded estimates of the number of pounds of blue crabs produced by the marginal (last) acre of wetlands. These estimates multiplied by the market price for crabs yielded a measure of the economic value of the marginal acre of wetland in production of crabs. Using this estimate, the analyst can infer the value changes associated with small alterations in wetland acreage.

The NFI technique can be used to estimate changes in economic values only if it can be assumed that the changes that wetland alteration will cause in production of the market good will not affect the market price of that good or the prices of any other production inputs. This assumption is realistic if the production decrease is small relative to the overall production of the market good, and reduces the total demand for production inputs by only a negligible amount. However, if wetland loss significantly lowers the entire market supply of the good (i.e., raises the cost of producing any given level of output), the equilibrium market price and output level will change. This complicates the analysis considerably because it requires an examination of how the entire market, including both consumers and producers, would react to the change in the wetland input. In other words, estimation of the changes in economic value associated with a change in the nature and supply of the intermediate wetland good requires knowledge of production and demand in the entire market for the final good both before and after the change. This type of estimation thus uses not only the NFI method, but market analysis going beyond that method.

To illustrate the kind of knowledge needed, consider a hypothetical alteration of a wetland ecosystem that is important to a nearby shrimp fishery which accounts for a significant share of total shrimp production. If the alteration reduces the shrimp population so much that the cost of producing any given level of shrimp increases, the market price and output of shrimp will also change. In turn, this will change consumers' WTP (consumer surplus) and producers' profits (economic rents). Because the demand for fish products is generally stable over a wide range of prices, shifts in the supply of shrimp may cause large fluctuations in price, but not in demand. The wetland alteration therefore could have the unexpected result of *increasing* returns to producers (because the large price rise would outweigh the reduction in sales). However, this does not mean that the wetland alteration would increase overall net social benefits associated with the shrimp fishery. On the contrary, the price rise could lower consumer surplus more than it raises economic rents, thus decreasing total net benefits. To estimate the overall change in the value of the wetland as a factor in shrimp production, one must consider the change in its value to both producers and consumers.

### Valuation of Final Wetland Goods

Final wetland goods include recreational opportunities and aesthetics. The appropriate measure of the value of these goods is the public's aggregate net WTP for them. Three techniques that may be used to measure this WTP are discussed below. Two of these, the travel cost and hedonic pricing methods, estimate net benefits indirectly using data on market expenditures for related goods. In contrast, the contingent valuation technique estimates net WTP directly by questioning users.

□ *Travel Cost (TC) Method.* The TC method is the oldest technique available for estimating the value of recreational benefits. In the wetlands context, it was applied as early as 1971 to value waterfowl hunting in Minnesota wetlands.[9] It is built on the hypothesis that public demand for recreational use of natural resources is indirectly reflected in travel and related expenditures incurred to visit natural sites. In other words, it assumes that the use or economic value of a recreational site is indirectly related to the costs of getting there.

The simplest version of the TC method, the single site model, determines consumer demand for the recreational uses of a site by plotting the rate of site visitation against the costs of that visitation. The model produces a demand relationship for recreational trips to a site as a function of simulated price, represented by travel costs and the value of the resource users' time. From this demand relationship, one can estimate consumers' net WTP to use the study site.

Application of the simple TC method involves several steps. First, the area surrounding the study site is divided into concentric zones, and the travel costs from each zone are estimated. Site visitors are surveyed to find their zones of origin, and a visitation rate (typically in visitor days per capita) for each zone is calculated using the survey data. These rates are summed to serve as one point on the site demand curve; this represents the aggregate use of the site at a zero price. The rates are regressed against travel costs and user socioeconomic characteristics to find their relationships to these variables. Other points on the demand curve are found by assuming that visitors would respond to a $1 increase in the price of site use just as they would to a $1 increase in travel costs, and using the visitation equation parameters to assess use at higher and higher travel costs. The consumers' net WTP for use of the site can be derived from this demand relationship.

The simple TC method requires site-specific data on the number of trips made from each zone, travel times, users' socioeconomic characteristics, and site entry fees. If other sites compete with the study site, the calculation must consider the possibility that a price rise at the study site will simply shift users to the competing sites. Otherwise, the calculation will overvalue the study site. This problem may be handled by including the travel costs and distances associated with competing sites as independent variables in the study site demand equation. The equation then specifies the demand for the study site as a function of substitute prices as well as of the site's own price.

This model assumes that all travel costs are tied to the demand for recreational services at the study site; thus trips to that site may not have multiple destinations. Also, distances traveled must vary enough to affect travel costs or the number of trips made, because estimation of a functional relationship between travel costs and visits requires observation of various cost/visit points. Therefore, the TC method is not well-suited to valuation of recreational sites close to major urban areas where the costs of visiting the site are likely to be relatively similar for a majority of users.

The simple TC method can be used to value the recreational goods provided by wetlands. It will produce order-of-magnitude approximations of total recreational use value at study sites. The model can be used to measure value changes resulting from site alterations, however, only if one assumes that changes in site quality can be described as changes in the effective quantity of site services available or in the price of those services.

A much more complicated TC model could measure value changes without making this assumption by incorporating site quality measures and their effects on the demand for recreational goods at the site. Site quality measures—measures of water quality, for example—would be independent variables in the model specification. If a site measure changed, the resulting change in use value could then be described as a shift in the demand function for the site. Recreational service quality measures such as "fisherman success rate" could also be included as variables in the TC equation. If the effects that changes in site quality will have on these variables can be predicted, the resulting shifts in demand for site services could be estimated.[10] However, this type of estimation requires (1) biological assessment of the effects of site alteration on site attributes, (2) knowledge of the relationship between site attributes and recreational quality indices, and (3) knowledge of the effects of recreational quality changes on visitation rates.

☐ *Hedonic Pricing—Property Value (PV) Analysis.* The hedonic group of valuation methods is based on the concept that since consumers ultimately derive satisfaction from the characteristics or attributes of commodities, the prices paid for market commodities are directly related to the nature and supply of these attributes. The most common hedonic technique relies on variations in property values to reveal implicit prices for environmental amenities; it uses these implicit prices to construct demand functions for the amenities. The PV approach generally is applicable only to those natural resource goods most likely to be captured by land values. For example, it has been used to value air quality[11] and aesthetics associated with proximity to open shoreline.[12]

The PV approach takes two steps to estimate the value of a resource good such as clean air. In the first step, a regression is constructed with property value as the dependent variable. The independent variables are quality/quantity indices of different property characteristics (e.g., number of rooms, proximity to schools, index of air quality), as well as household socioeconomic characteristics. The estimated parameters represent the implicit marginal prices of these characteristics, that is, individuals' marginal WTP for each of them. If the estimated equation is nonlinear, these implicit prices will vary across individual observations. In the second step, the implicit price of air quality is used to construct a demand relationship from which a use value measure may be estimated.

The conceptual and empirical complexities of the PV approach limit its usefulness in valuing wetland goods. The most troublesome empirical problem involves the second-stage construction of demand relationships from estimated implicit prices. Thibodeau and Ostro sidestep this second stage[13] in their study of the value of the open space service provided by Massachusetts wetlands. They use a linear equation in the first stage to estimate a constant implicit price for proximity of open space, and use this price to estimate the value of this wetland service for adjacent homes. While this approach does not estimate net WTP, it may be useful for estimating gross approximations of the use value of wetland services, such as proximity to open space. It requires cross-section or time-series data on property values and property and household characteristics for a well-defined market area that includes homes abutting as well as those farther away from the wetland.

Measurement of the value changes associated with changes in wetland services generally requires second-stage estimation, although approximation of the value changes associated with small, incremental changes in wetland services may only require implicit price information derived from first-stage estimation. Measurement of any value changes, however, requires knowledge of the new level of the wetland good, and therefore knowledge of the physical production and transformation functions determining that level.

☐ *Contingent Valuation (CV) Method.* Contingent valuation estimates net benefits by questioning consumers directly about their valuation of nonmarket goods. It thus provides an alternative to the indirect valuation approaches that rely on market data to estimate the economic value of such goods. Although CV could theoretically be used to estimate the societal benefits provided by any nonmarket wetland good, it is best suited to goods that are easily identified and understood by users and that are consumed in discrete units (e.g., recreational goods). CV is the only available technique for estimating most types of nonuse values.[14]

The cornerstone of the CV approach is that, given appropriate assumptions, consumers can reveal their net WTP for nonmarket goods through hypothetical market transactions. The method assumes that people understand the good in question and will reveal their preferences in the contingent market just as they would in a real market. CV studies rely on mail surveys or personal interviews that use direct questions, bidding games, or payment cards to elicit WTP-revealing responses. Careful administration of a properly designed survey questionnaire to a representative sample of resource users yields an order-of-magnitude approximation of the representative user's net WTP for a season or day of site use. Coupled with data on the total number of resource users, this approximation can be used to estimate the total use value of the resource good.

Design and administration of the survey questionnaire are the most important and difficult aspects of a CV study. The survey instrument must be carefully constructed and administered to portray the resource good accurately and to eliminate potential biases in consumer responses. CV has drawn criticism because consumers' answers to hypothetical questions may be inherently biased, and even bias-free answers may not reveal how the consumers would actually behave in practice. One potential bias involves strategic behavior: consumers seeking to maximize private well-being may intentionally attempt to influence policy by over- or understating their true WTP. Other potential biases may result from incomplete information on the hypothetical situation (e.g., information on substitute activities, resource characteristics, etc.), from vehicle bias (how the respondents are made to believe they would have to pay), or from starting point bias (the dollar amount at which bidding starts in bidding games). In general, these biases can be addressed through careful design and administration of the survey instrument. A more important potential problem is that even bias-free answers in hypothetical experiments may not reveal how resource users would actually behave in practice. While this is always a potential problem, recent studies have shown that CV estimates of resource good use values are comparable to those produced by the TC approach.[15]

A CV questionnaire would need to be more sophisticated to estimate the effects of site alteration on the benefits provided by a recreational service. Specifically, the questionnaire would need to show respondents how alteration would affect recreational good quantity and/or quality. To adequately develop this changing service flow scenario, the survey designer would need to know the physical and economic linkages underlying the production of recreational services at the site.

□ *Valuation Transfers: The Activity Day Method.* The economics-based methods for estimating the use value of nonmarket recreational goods often cannot be applied in the context of federal water resource decisionmaking because of data limitations and/or resource constraints. When this is the case, it may be useful to apply economic-based models or unit values previously developed for goods at other sites. Such valuation "transfers" permit inference of the value of similar goods at the study site.

There are two types of valuation transfers. A simple transfer might use an activity day value (e.g., the value of a user day of duck hunting) previously developed at another site to value this activity at the study site. For example, an estimate of net WTP for a user day of trout fishing might be derived from a TC study at another site and applied to value trout fishing at the study site. Multiplying this activity day value by the estimated annual number of user days available for the activity at the study site produces a use value estimate for the good at that site. Recreation participation data are available from the U.S. Fish and Wildlife Service, and are also often gathered by state and local wildlife and recreation agencies.

A better but much more complicated transfer might apply a valuation model derived from a previous TC study to the resource good and user characteristics of the study site. Such a model might use a regression equation relating net WTP for recreational site use (the dependent variable) to independent variables, such as user characteristics, distances traveled to the site, and site quality indices. If values for these independent variables can be developed for the study site, the regression equation parameter estimates can be used to predict the net WTP for site use of users traveling from varying distances. This information, coupled with an estimate of the number of recreational user days, provides an estimate of recreational use value for the study site. This type of advanced valuation transfer often is not cost-effective, because implementing it requires almost as much data as conducting a TC study at the site itself. The remainder of this section focuses only on simple valuation transfers using activity day values.

Recreation activity day values represent values accruing to actual users of a recreational good at a particular site. They are therefore based on a myriad of site-specific factors, including the following:

- site quality factors for recreational activities (e.g., water quality, type of game fish available);
- locational factors (e.g., distance from user populations, number of close substitutes in the region); and
- user populations' socioeconomic and other characteristics.

Because activity day values are site/location/user specific, their cross-application to estimate the use values of comparable recreational activities at different sites is deficient unless the sites share all of these characteristics. That is, when these variables differ across sites, unit values for recreation activities at the sites will vary. Nevertheless, unit values may prove very useful for making gross estimates of recreational values because they can be easily and quickly cross-applied. Moreover, some of the biases resulting from cross-application of site-specific estimates can be minimized by using estimates derived for sites with characteristics corresponding to those of the study site.

Past applications of the TC and CV methods to particular recreation sites have produced numerous activity day value estimates that might be cross-applied to wetland areas. These estimates are available for many different recreation activities in many different locations. For example, two recent federal government publications review activity day values for particular types of recreational activities in specific areas (typically states). The values represent estimates of the average consumer surplus (use value) accruing to an individual user for a day of an activity at a site. These estimates provide enough data on recreational values to allow application of simple unit value transfers for many common recreational activities in many parts of the country.

The first of these publications, prepared in 1984 by the U.S. Forest Service,[16] attempted to pull together and standardize the results of previous research efforts that estimated unit values for a wide variety of recreation activities using the TC and CV methodologies. The authors converted these results into activity values per user day. They also tried to adjust the values to correct for methodological differences among the studies, so that the remaining differences in value estimates for some recreational activity at different sites reflect only differences in site-specific factors, such as site quality and user characteristics. The publication includes activity day values for the following recreation activities in many areas of the United States: anadromous fishing, big game hunting, camping, hiking, cold water fishing, warm water fishing, waterfowl hunting, nonmotorized boating, picnicking, and wilderness experience.

The second publication, a 1987 working paper prepared by the U.S. Fish and Wildlife Service,[17] sets out activity day values for waterfowl hunting, deer hunting, and trout fishing for every state. These value estimates are based on the 1980 National Survey of Fishing, Hunting and Wildlife Associated Recreation.[18] That survey gathered extensive data on participation in and expenditures for wildlife-associated recreation, as well as on participants' socioeconomic characteristics and on other aspects of their recreational activities. The Survey also asked a series of CV questions to determine respondents' net WTP for fishing and hunting. The activity day value estimates in the 1987 publication are based on the responses to these questions. Each estimate represents the average net WTP for a user day of a specific fishing or hunting activity in a given state.

Activity day value estimates representing the average net WTP of individual users may also be used to predict the recreational value changes that will result from significant site alterations. However, these predictions require estimates of activity day values both before and after site alteration, as well as of the effects of the alteration on participation in the activity at the site.

*Valuation of Intermediate Wetland Services: Damage Prevention Inputs*

The preceding sections focused on the use of WTP-based methods to value final wetland services and intermediate wetland services that contribute to commercial production. In contrast, some of the damage prevention services that wetlands provide (e.g., flood control, erosion prevention, and pollution assimilation) typically are not amenable to valuation through estimation of the public's net WTP for them. Although some of these services may contribute to the production of market goods, they may not be amenable to NFI valuation because no economic profits are associated with those goods. For example, a wetland may be used for tertiary treatment of human wastes. However, this type of final municipal good is often not competitively priced, but rather supplied at below cost. Therefore, it generates no economic profit from which to infer the value of the wetland service. Similarly, most nonmarket damage prevention services cannot be valued using the indirect techniques discussed above. The TC method is inapplicable because use of damage prevention services generally is not associated with expenditures on market goods. The PV method is inappropriate because property owners and buyers are unlikely to fully understand the damage prevention services provided by nearby wetlands, so property prices will not reflect the value of those services. Similarly, CV is difficult to apply because damage prevention is not easily understood by users or consumed in discrete units. Our inability to derive economic measures of value for damage prevention services presents a major problem for wetland valuation: finding surrogate measures of value that are as consistent as possible with the economic concept of use value.

Two such approaches may be used to value wetland damage prevention services: the replacement cost and damage cost methods.

These approaches essentially estimate the costs of alternatives to wetland damage prevention services. Because they do not explicitly consider society's preferences for wetland services or consumer and producer behavior absent those services, they are not consistent with economic principles of benefit assessment. Nevertheless, under certain conditions, they produce value estimates that may be used as gross approximations of WTP.

☐ *Replacement Cost (RC) Method.* The RC approach estimates the value of a nonmarket environmental service based on the cost of providing it through an alternative supply mechanism, typically a technological substitute. For example, to value the waste assimilation service provided by a wetland area, one might ascertain the cost of building and operating a tertiary waste treatment system that could provide the same service.

The basic RC methodology involves three steps. The first step is estimating the level of the environmental service provided. For some services, such as flood control, this might mean conducting an ecological assessment. For others, such as domestic water supply, it might simply involve investigating use level directly (e.g., determining how much of the nearby domestic water supply comes from wetland wells). The second step is identifying the least cost alternative supply mechanism that could provide the same benefit level. This step is necessary because the public would not be willing to pay any more for the service than it must. The step requires conducting engineering and cost assessments of the various alternative supply mechanisms. For example, it might involve calculating the feasibility and cost of obtaining water from secondary sources, such as nearby water districts. The third step is gathering evidence that the public would demand the identified least cost supply mechanism, at its price, in lieu of the wetland service.[19] Without this evidence, the RC method will overstate the public's net WTP for the wetland service.

The deficiency of the RC approach lies in the difficulty of its third step. Net WTP for any good is determined by existing supply *and demand* conditions. The first two steps of the RC method reflect only supply, not demand. However, if a wetland service were eliminated, the public would not necessarily be willing to pay for the identified least cost alternative merely because it would supply the same benefit level as that service. Without evidence that the public would demand the alternative, this methodology is not an economically appropriate estimator of wetland service value.

To measure the value change associated with a specific proposed wetland alteration, assessment of the least cost alternative supply mechanism must be keyed to that alteration. This requires a determination of how the alteration would affect the wetland service level, which in turn requires knowledge or assumptions about the physical production and transformation linkages underlying the service.

☐ *Damage Cost (DC) Method.* The DC method estimates the value of a wetland service based on the cost of the damage that might result from its loss. For example, the wetland service of erosion prevention may be valued based on the cost of removing sediment from a navigable waterway. Gupta and Foster[20] and Thibodeau and Ostro[21] valued the flood control benefits provided by Massachusetts wetlands based on estimates of the property damage expected to occur without them.

Several steps are involved in estimating the dollar amount of business and property damage that might result from elimination of a wetland service. First, an ecological assessment of the service level is necessary to determine the physical impact of eliminating it. Second, the potential physical damage to property, either annually or over some discrete time period, must be estimated. Third, this damage must be translated into dollar terms. Fourth, an RC-type investigation of alternative supply mechanisms must be conducted, because a DC value estimate should be used only if no substitute supply mechanism could provide the wetland service at a price lower than that estimate.

The DC method shares the defect of the RC method: it does not consider social preferences for wetland services or individuals' behavior in the absence of those services. For example, if development eliminates the flood control function of a particular wetland ecosystem, nearby property owners may be willing to pay for structural measures to avert some or all of the effects of increased flooding rather than risk property damage. In such a case, the full cost of the flood damages expected absent this behavior would exceed the benefits provided by the wetland's flood control function. For this reason, the DC method should be used only as a last resort to value wetland services, and DC values should be viewed as gross upper bound benefit estimates.

Like the RC method, the DC method may be used to estimate the use value changes associated with a specific proposed wetland alteration if it is keyed to that alteration. The physical linkages underlying production of a service must be identified in order to predict the effect of the alteration on the service level.

☐ *Energy Analysis/Biological Productivity Method.* A few wetland ecologists have developed and advocated another wetland valuation method that is based on the energy content of the natural environment instead of on consumer preferences for wetland goods. This method is called the energy analysis (EA) or biological productivity approach. It originated in the belief of many ecologists that traditional economic analysis vastly underestimates the benefits that wetlands provide to society.[22] These ecologists argue that the "component" approach to valuation of wetland goods neglects wetlands' total "life-support" value, or primary productivity.

The EA approach rests on the assumption that the value of any good is reflected in the amount of energy required to produce it.[23] If energy is defined as the basic input into all production, wetlands may be valued by their biomass energy, that is, by the biological productivity that supports the services they provide. Wetland value can therefore be calculated by multiplying a wetland's total units of energy (measured in calories of biomass) by some energy price.

The first major application of the EA method was to coastal wetlands in the southeastern United States.[24] This study used the annual net production of salt marshes to represent the energy flow of wetlands that carry out various functions. It used a conversion factor of 1850 kilocalories/pound of biomass to estimate kilocalories per acre, then applied an equivalence factor of 104 kilocalories/dollar. The total life-support value per acre was found to be $4,100 annually.

Since the EA approach assumes that values of wetland goods are determined by the amount of available energy, it is incompatible with the postulates of economic theory. Specifically, EA neglects the role of consumer demand in determination of value, assuming that society's objective is to maximize net energy instead of consumer satisfaction.[25] This cost-of-supply approach to valuation is incompatible with an economic system that determines value by the interaction of supply and demand.

## Other Concepts Related to Valuation of Nonmarket Goods

The following sections review other economic concepts related to the valuation of nonmarket goods. These concepts include the nonuse values of natural environments, such as wetlands, and the secondary impacts of water development.

### Nonuse (Intrinsic) Value

The economic value of wetland goods has been defined as the public's aggregate WTP to use these goods, above what it actually does pay. However, people may also be willing to pay to preserve natural resources even if they do not presently use their services. Economists refer to this preservation value as nonuse or intrinsic value.

Economists recognize two types of nonuse value—existence value and option value. Existence value is the amount that present generations would be willing to pay to preserve a natural resource even if they never plan to use its services. Thus, this value may be independent of both present and future uses of the resource. For example, people may be willing to pay to ensure that blue whales continue to exist even though they never expect to see one. The existence of the whales may give people direct satisfaction as well as the vicarious satisfaction of knowing that their children will have the opportunity to enjoy these unique resources. The existence of resource conservation and environmental groups suggests that, at least on an aggregate level, society is willing to pay to preserve unique and irreplaceable resources. The existence value of unique ecological systems or resources may be substantial.

Option value exists when individuals not presently using a service wish to keep the option of using it later.[26] It is the difference between the value these individuals obtain from current use of a resource and the amount they are willing to pay for the right to use it in the future.[27] In essence, it is the risk premium that the individuals would be willing to pay to preserve the option of using the resource in the face of uncertainty about future supply and demand. Option value is positive when the future availability of a resource is uncertain[28] or when its use is uncertain because of exogenous factors (reasons other than uncertainty regarding future income or price).[29]

Existence and option values are relatively new economic concepts. It is generally agreed that they exist and can be substantial for the goods and services provided by unique and irreplaceable natural environments. However, only a few attempts have been made to estimate them. CV is currently the only technique capable of eliciting most of these values. It has been used primarily to estimate intrinsic values of wildlife resources[30] and wilderness.[31]

*Secondary Impacts*

When water resource development reduces public and commercial wetland use, local and regional economic impacts may result that are not accounted for in the changed use values of wetland goods. For example, elimination of a fishery may result in unemployment of fishermen and reduction of expenditures at local fishing-related businesses. Should these impacts be treated as societal economic losses attributable to wetlands development? That is, should wetlands-related employment and expenditures be included in wetlands' use value to society?

The economic concept of *opportunity costs* generally dictates negative answers to these questions. An opportunity cost is the worth of a resource in its next best alternative use, that is, the payment the resource would receive in that use which is sacrificed by keeping it in its present use. Because of opportunity costs, inputs displaced by wetlands development will logically move into other uses.

Consider the case of a wetland ecosystem that contributes to a nearby commercial fishery by supporting the aquatic food chain and providing a spawning and nursery ground. If a water resource project negatively affects the wetland, and this in turn affects fishery production, the economic impact would be measured by changes in the economic rents and consumer surplus accruing to producers and consumers of fishery products. The change in production might also reduce the number of laborers employed on commercial fishing vessels. However, because opportunity costs exist for these laborers, the employment effects should not be counted as part of the economic impact on the fishery. That is, if the displaced laborers have alternative employment opportunities, their loss of employment in the fishery is not real economic loss. To consider their values part of the fishery's value would imply that they have no value in any alternative employment (zero opportunity costs). Similarly, a reduction in commercial fishing may result in reduced expenditures on fishing gear and tackle. These lost expenditures should not be treated as economic losses because they will be redistributed to other goods and services. From a national welfare standpoint, a redistribution of expenditures among inputs cannot be considered economic loss.

This conclusion requires two qualifications. The first relates to the transaction costs of moving inputs into new uses. Transaction costs may include costs of relocating inputs, obtaining permits, training in new skills, or even relinquishing traditions. Transaction costs reduce opportunity costs and represent real economic loss. The second qualification involves local and regional perspectives. In general, calculations of social economic loss should exclude secondary impacts because they will cancel out for the nation as a whole (for example, expenditures lost in one area will be gained in others). However, these impacts can be important to local and regional economies.

## Economic Barriers to Valuation of Wetlands

The economic technology for valuing the nonmarket outputs of natural ecosystems has developed tremendously over the last 20 years. While still far from perfect, the state of the art now makes it possible to approximate the monetary value of the benefits provided by a wide range of natural resource characteristics, including benefits previously treated as "intangibles." Using this new technology, policymakers can better assess the societal value of wetland ecosystems.

Ideally, systems models should be developed that combine economic techniques with interactive scientific data on the biological and physical relationships linking wetland characteristics to wetland outputs. This bioeconomic modeling would permit quantification of the relationships among wetland characteristics, quantity and quality of wetland outputs, and human use and societal value of those outputs. If such systems modeling could be done for regional wetland areas, the value of many regional wetland benefits could be assessed. Given predictions on how development might affect wetland characteristics, the model could be used to predict the value of the resulting marginal changes in benefits.

Unfortunately, such bioeconomic wetland valuation models are not currently available, and are not likely to be in the near future. Some of the obstacles to their development are their complexity, extensive data requirements, and costs. Perhaps the greatest obstacle, however, is our limited scientific understanding of the linkages among wetland characteristics, functions, and outputs. Scientific limitations make comprehensive wetland valuation difficult in two ways. First, wetland services can only be valued if they can be detected, and science cannot yet detect some of them. Second, we lack quantified linkages that would allow us to predict how proposed development might affect wetland output quantity and quality. This makes it impossible to use economics to estimate the resulting changes in output use and value.

Given the existing economic and scientific barriers, wetlands must be valued using a second-best approach. This approach involves identifying regional wetland outputs that are readily apparent and/or generally recognized by the scientific community and applying available economic techniques to estimate their current values. The outputs can be identified by observing types and levels of wetland use, and the economic techniques to be applied are those described in this chapter.

This approach will yield lower bound estimates of the wetland values that water resource development might diminish or eliminate.

---

Despite its limitations, economics is capable of playing a much greater role in wetlands valuation than it has to date. The next chapter explains how and why the federal approaches to wetlands valuation fail to use available economic tools. Chapter Five discusses the legislative response in another area where science and economics face valuation difficulties—the assessment of natural resource damages—and considers the lessons this approach may offer for wetlands valuation. Chapter Six suggests some steps toward optimal use of economic tools in wetlands valuation.

## Notes to Chapter 3

1. This discussion suggests that the optimal or economically efficient level of wetland resources would be ensured if owners could charge for the benefits these resources provide to society. However, any non-zero price charged for such benefits would itself cause allocation inefficiencies because it would discourage some use of wetland goods, which is undesirable since the marginal cost of providing these goods to additional users is zero. Since the optimal prices for wetland goods are positive for wetland owners, but zero for users, the marketplace is incapable of setting an equilibrium price for wetlands that can ensure their efficient level and use.

2. Although consumption of the market good also generates consumer surplus, this surplus cannot be attributed entirely to the wetland input, because it is the result of all inputs combined.

3. In many instances the first two steps can be combined.

4. J. LEITCH, SOCIOECONOMIC VALUES OF WETLANDS: CONCEPTS, RESEARCH METHODS, AND ANNOTATED BIBLIOGRAPHY (North Dakota Research Report No. 81, North Dakota Agricultural Experiment Station, North Dakota State University, 1981); Larson, *Evaluation Models for Public Management of Freshwater Wetlands,* in TRANSACTIONS OF THE FORTIETH NORTH AMERICAN WILDLIFE AND NATURAL RESOURCES CONFERENCE 40 (1975); Whisler, *Management of Wetlands for Agricultural Production, Water Storage and Recycling: Alternative Uses,* in WATER RESOURCES UTILIZATION AND CONSERVATION IN THE ENVIRONMENT (Fort Valley State College, 1974).

5. For a more technical discussion of these methods, see E. YANG, R. DOWER & M. MENEFEE, THE USE OF ECONOMIC ANALYSIS FOR VALUING NATURAL RESOURCE DAMAGE (1984). A more detailed discussion of the data needs and potential applications and limitations of these techniques may be found in W. DESVOUSGES & J. SKAHEN, TECHNIQUES TO MEASURE DAMAGES TO NATURAL RESOURCES (1985).

6. Lynne, Conroy & Prochaska, *Economic Valuation of Marsh Areas for Marine Production Processes,* 8 J. ENVTL. ECON. & MGMT. 175 (1981).

7. S. BATIE & J. WILSON, ECONOMIC VALUES ATTRIBUTABLE TO VIRGINIA'S COASTAL WETLAND AS INPUTS IN OYSTER PRODUCTION (U.S. Dep't of Agricultural Economics Research Division Bulletin 150, Virginia Polytechnic and State University, 1979).

8. *See, e.g.,* Tihensky & Meade, *Establishing the Economic Value of Estuaries to U.S. Commercial Fisheries,* in PROCEEDINGS OF ESTUARINE POLLUTION CONTROL AND MEASUREMENT 671 (U.S. Environmental Protection Agency, 1975).

9. J. GOLDSTEIN, COMPETITION FOR WETLANDS IN THE MIDWEST: AN ECONOMIC ANALYSIS (1971).

10. *See* Freeman, *Approaches to Measuring Public Goods Demands,* 61 AM. J. AGRIC. ECON. (Dec. 1979).

11. Harrison & Rubinfeld, *Hedonic Housing Prices and the Demand for Clean Air,* 5 J. ENVTL. ECON. & MGMT. 81 (1978).

12. Brown & Pollakowski, *Economic Valuation of Shoreline,* 59 REV. ECON. & STATISTICS 272 (1977).

13. Thibodeau & Ostro, *An Economic Analysis of Wetland Protection,* 12 J. ENVTL. MGMT. 19 (1981).

14. *See infra* pp. 42-43.

15. *See, e.g.,* Sellar, Stoll & Chavas, *Validation of Empirical Measures of Wetland Change: A Comparison of Nonmarket Techniques,* 61 LAND ECON. 156 (1985).

16. C. SORG & J. LOOMIS, EMPIRICAL ESTIMATES OF AMENITY FOREST VALUES: A COMPARATIVE REVIEW (General Technical Report RM-107, (U.S. Forest Service, U.S. Dep't of Agriculture, 1984).

17. G. BROWN & M. HAY, NET ECONOMIC RECREATION VALUE FOR DEER AND WATERFOWL HUNTING AND TROUT FISHING, 1980 (Working Paper No. 23, Division of Policy and Directives Management, U.S. Fish and Wildlife Service, 1987).

18. U.S. FISH AND WILDLIFE SERVICE, U.S. DEP'T OF INTERIOR, THE 1980 NATIONAL SURVEY OF FISHING, HUNTING, AND WILDLIFE ASSOCIATED RECREATION (1982).

19. S. Batie & L. Shabman, Using Replacement Cost Measures of Economic Value in Wetlands Management (Paper Prepared for Agricultural Economics Association Meeting, Logan, Utah, Aug. 1982).

20. Gupta & Foster, *Economic Criteria for Freshwater Wetland Policy in Massachusetts,* 57 AM. J. AGRIC. ECON. 40 (1975).

21. Thibodeau & Ostro, *supra* note 13.

22. J. GOSSELINK, E. ODUM & R. POPE, THE VALUE OF TIDAL MARSH (Publication No. LSU-56-74-03, Center for Wetland Resources, Louisiana State University, 1974).

23. J. ODUM & E. ODUM, ENERGY BASIS FOR MAN AND NATURE (1976).

24. J. GOSSELINK *et al., supra* note 22.

25. Shabman & Batie, *Economic Value of Natural Coastal Wetlands: A Critique,* 4 COASTAL ZONE MGMT. J. 231 (1978).

26. Weisbrod, *Collective-Consumption Services of Individual Consumption Goods,* 78 Q.J. ECON. 528 (1964).

27. Cicchetti & Freeman, *Option Demand and Consumer Surplus: Further Comments,* 85 Q.J. ECON. 528 (1971).

28. Bishop, *Option Value: An Exposition and Extension,* 58 LAND ECON. 1 (1982).

29. Freeman, *The Sign and Size of Option Value,* 60 LAND ECON. 1 (1984).

30. Brookshire, Eubankes & Randall, *Estimating Option Prices and Existence Values for Wildlife Resources,* 59 LAND ECON. 1 (1983).

31. Walsh, Loomis & Gillman, *Valuing Option, Existence, and Bequest Demands for Wilderness,* 60 LAND ECON. 14 (1984).

# Chapter 4:
# The Implementation of
# Wetland Valuation

T he U.S. Army Corps of Engineers is the primary federal construction agency for major public works programs that develop
water and water-related land resources.[1] Because many wetlands are
located in or hydrologically connected to waters subject to such development, Corps decisions can have substantial impacts on wetland use.
Statutes and regulations require the Corps to assess and consider
adverse impacts on wetlands when it plans and evaluates projects. To
a significant degree, the manner in which the Corps fulfills these duties
determines the extent of wetland preservation in the United States.

This chapter examines how the Corps' decisionmaking accounts
for the economic impacts of wetland loss and degradation. The discussion illustrates one approach that the federal government has taken
in seeking to compensate for the market's inability to allocate wetland
resources properly. The chapter first identifies the types of Corps projects that can adversely affect wetlands and describes some of their
impacts. It then examines the Corps' process of reaching decisions
on these projects and the way in which this process factors in wetland
economic values. This discussion focuses on the Corps' use of benefit-
cost analysis. It reviews both the guidelines that the Corps follows
and the methodologies that it uses in accounting for the benefits and
costs of its projects, particularly in monetizing or otherwise considering environmental costs. The chapter concludes that federal water
resource development decisions generally have not taken advantage
of state-of-the-art techniques for assessing and valuing impacts on
wetlands.[2]

## Some Corps Water Projects and Their Potential Wetland Impacts

The Corps is responsible for constructing most federal river and harbor projects.[3] Each such project must be both authorized and funded by Congress. As of 1985, the Corps listed 371 authorized "active" water projects with a total estimated cost of $18.9 billion and 540 "inactive" or deferred projects with a total estimated cost of $17.3 billion. However, 675 of these 911 projects had received no funding in 10 years.[4] The Water Resources Development Act of 1986[5] was the first congressional authorization of new water projects in over 10 years. It authorized $16 billion worth of new projects, including 115 flood control projects and 50 navigation projects. In August 1989, the Corps listed 518 active projects and 311 inactive or deferred projects, but many of these were listed as likely to be deauthorized. Actual construction of each authorized project will require a separate congressional appropriation.

Corps water projects are generally constructed and operated in or adjacent to rivers, lakes, and coastal waters. Both project construction and project operation may adversely affect adjacent and nearby wetland ecosystems. The impacts vary with project type and geographic location but can include both direct and indirect effects on wetland quantity and quality.

One major subset of Corps activities is dam construction and operation. Dams can seriously affect wetlands in several ways. For example, the waters impounded by dams can inundate and destroy upstream wetlands. Dam drawdown can affect upstream and downstream wetlands by altering normal seasonal flooding and by releasing water sporadically. Deepwater dam releases can negatively affect downstream wetlands by altering water temperature. Finally, flood control dams can indirectly affect the quality of nearby wetlands by creating an incentive for increased residential, commercial, and agricultural development.

Many Corps flood control dam projects have had significant wetland impacts. For example, the Pick-Sloan Program, begun in the 1940s, produced a series of flood control structures and channelization measures that eventually altered all but 50 miles of the Missouri River. The program's wetland impacts have included direct destruction of over 300,000 acres of terrestrial habitat, 100,000 acres of aquatic habitat, and 65,000 acres of islands and sandbars.[6] Corps flood control projects begun in the late 1920s on the Kissimmee River, Lake Okeechobee, and the Everglades in South and Central Florida have also had substantial wetland impacts. More than 140,000 acres of wetlands have been directly destroyed by drainage or indirectly affected by agricultural expansion into areas previously too wet to farm.

The projects have also facilitated urban expansion in floodplain areas along the Florida coast.[7]

Other important Corps activities are designed to maintain and improve navigation in and on inland waterways, intercoastal waterways, and ports and harbors. These projects include shipping locks, bulkheads, levees, revetments, pumping and drainage, dredging, and channelization. Their potential negative impacts on wetlands are numerous and immediate. Some of these impacts result from siltation. For example, channel deepening and straightening increase flow velocity, often causing severe erosion that results in siltation of downstream wetlands. This process may both damage existing wetlands and prevent development of new wetlands by inhibiting natural marsh accretion. In addition, passage of more and deeper-draft vessels in channelized waterways stirs up bottom sediments and erodes shorelines. The resulting silt can fill in backwater channels and freshwater wetlands.

Navigation improvement measures can also damage wetlands in other ways. For example, channel deepening and channelization involve dredging large quantities of spoil from waterway bottoms. The spoil must be disposed of in some manner, and often it is dumped into adjacent wetlands. Bulkheading, levee or revetment construction, and channel deepening and straightening may affect wetlands by causing water level fluctuations. Moreover, they often cut off the natural water supply of adjacent wetlands by imposing physical barriers or lowering water tables. For example, waterway channelization converts shallow water systems into deepwater habitats, frequently eliminating fringe wetlands by cutting off their water flow. Much of the marsh loss in the Mississippi River Valley has been attributed to significant channelization of the Mississippi and Red Rivers.[8] Channel dredging may also facilitate private and public drainage of "wet soils" by increasing waterway carrying capacity. In coastal areas, channel dredging can alter the natural gradual slope from the shoreline seaward, thus increasing the impact on wetlands of waves and storms.

## Benefit-Cost Analysis of Corps Water Projects: The WRC Guidelines

Congress will not appropriate funds for a Corps water project unless a current evaluation shows that its expected national benefits outweigh its estimated costs.[9] The Corps therefore subjects each alternative project plan to a test comparing its estimated dollar benefits to society with its estimated dollar costs. Benefits are divided by costs, and a project is deemed to be in the national interest if the resulting benefit-cost ratio is greater than one-to-one.[10] In conducting these benefit-cost analyses, the Corps follows guidelines developed by the Water Resources Council (WRC). These guidelines set out procedures for quantifying and evaluating the benefits and costs of project alternatives; they specify the benefit and cost categories to be considered and the particular dollar quantification methodologies to be used.

The following section traces the history of the use of benefit-cost analysis in water resource development decisions, focusing on consideration of environmental factors. The subsequent section reviews the content and use of the WRC Guidelines, focusing on the ways in which they factor wetland impacts and other cost and benefit components into project planning and evaluation.

*History of the Guidelines*

The Corps has been using benefit-cost analysis to determine the economic desirability of proposed water projects since passage of the Flood Control Act of 1936.[11] This Act provided that the federal government could participate in the improvement of navigable waters for flood control purposes if "the benefits to whomsoever they may accrue are in excess of the estimated costs." Although this benefit-cost requirement applied only to Corps and Department of Agriculture flood control projects, all federal water resource agencies soon began applying benefit-cost analysis to all their water projects. After World War II, benefit-cost analysis became the principal basis of project recommendations by federal water agencies. Each agency used its own procedures and methodologies to evaluate the benefits and costs of its respective projects. The agencies were generally consistent, however, in one important respect. They all evaluated project alternatives in terms of the monetized benefits resulting from the expected increase in goods and services (or decrease in the cost of producing a given level of goods and services) and the estimated costs of constructing, operating, and maintaining the project.

At the request of President Kennedy in 1962, an ad hoc interagency commission on water resources established a set of directives to guide the formulation and evaluation of all federal water project plans. This set of directives, known as Senate Document 97, articulated four water resource planning objectives: national economic development, regional economic development, preservation of natural resources, and general human well-being. Senate Document 97 recommended that agencies consider all these objectives when planning and evaluating proposed water projects. Accordingly, it recommended that project plans fully describe their "secondary" benefits (e.g., local and regional income and employment effects) and their "intangible" benefits (e.g., enhancement of environmental quality). These benefits were not to affect project justification, however. The favorable benefit-cost comparison required to justify a project involved only tangible national economic development accounts.

Many contended that Senate Document 97 "liberalized" water project benefit-cost justification by allowing federal agencies to show monetized secondary and intangible benefits, even if those benefits did not directly weigh into the benefit-cost balance.[12] It was also argued, however, that project decisionmakers did not give environmental and economic impacts equal consideration because natural resource values that would be foregone with development were not amenable to monetary evaluation.[13]

In 1965, the Water Resources Planning Act established the WRC, comprised of the secretaries of several cabinet departments and the chairman of the Federal Power Commission.[14] The WRC's purposes were to survey national and regional water resource management needs and to ensure uniform and consistent formulation and evaluation of federal water project plans. In 1968, the Senate and House Public Works Committees requested the WRC to establish principles and procedures whereby federal water project planning and evaluation would give adequate weight to all project benefits, including regional benefits. Pursuant to this request, the WRC appointed a task force to review and revise Senate Document 97.[15] The task force recommended basing federal water resource planning on essentially the same objectives that Senate Document 97 outlined. However, it recommended that all the objectives be somehow monetized or otherwise evaluated and be given *equal* weight in project planning and evaluation.

These recommendations were set out in a September 1973 WRC rulemaking, "Principles and Standards for Planning Water and Related Land Resources." The "Principles and Standards" established a broad policy framework for water resource planning. They provided rules to guide federal water resource agencies in formulating uniform and consistent procedures for measuring and comparing the beneficial and adverse effects of alternative project plans. However, they gave the various agencies responsibility for actually establishing these procedures. Moreover, they gave the agencies no guidance on how to monetize or otherwise quantify environmental costs. Throughout the

1970s, therefore, federal agencies continued to rely on different and often inconsistent criteria for quantifying and evaluating the expected benefits and costs of alternative water project plans.

In response to this continuing problem, President Carter in July 1978 issued a memorandum, "Improvements in the Planning and Evaluation of Water Resources Programs and Projects." The President expressed concern that environmental costs and nonstructural alternatives received too little consideration in federal water project planning. The memorandum directed the WRC to evaluate current agency practices for quantifying expected project benefits and costs and to publish a planning manual to ensure that the best available procedures were used to estimate those benefits and costs. The directive thus entrusted the WRC with the job of developing a single set of procedures and methodologies for federal water agencies to use in monetizing or otherwise quantifying and evaluating water project benefits and costs, including environmental costs.

During 1979 and 1980, the WRC revised the "Principles and Standards" into final rules to guide quantification and evaluation of project benefits and costs. These rules mandated *equal* consideration of environmental quality and economic development objectives. This marked the first time that federal water resource agencies had been directed to consider environmental quality on a par with national economic development. The rules also set forth procedures and methodologies for federal agencies to use in quantifying the expected benefits and costs of project alternatives and in evaluating environmental quality effects that were not amenable to dollar valuation. The rules mandated consideration of nonstructural project alternatives and of ways in which alternative projects might affect the water resource plans of other federal agencies, such as the Fish and Wildlife Service.

The emphasis on considering environmental quality effects in planning and evaluating water projects decreased under the Reagan administration. In 1982, the WRC voted to replace the "Principles and Standards" with a set of guidelines for federal agencies. These new WRC Guidelines[16] retain the "Principles and Standards" methodologies for quantifying project benefits and costs. The Guidelines, however, are just that; federal agencies are not directed to follow the principles or use the methodologies set forth. In addition, the Guidelines delete the "Principles and Standards" requirement of equal consideration of environmental quality objectives.

## Content and Use of the Guidelines

Although they are not required to do so, all federal agencies, including the Corps, follow the WRC Guidelines when planning and evaluating water project alternatives.[17] The following discussion reviews and critiques the principles and methodologies set forth in the Guidelines, focusing on how the wetland impacts of project alternatives are quantified and factored into the benefit-cost balance.

The Guidelines articulate two water resource planning objectives: alleviation of water-related problems and contribution to national economic development (NED). NED is measured by net monetary value, calculated as project benefits minus project costs. Project benefits are defined as increases in national outputs of goods and services. Project costs are to include environmental goods and services foregone with development *to the extent that they can be monetized*. They are also to include the costs of measures to mitigate adverse project effects.

In evaluating the Guidelines and their implementation, it is critical to note that they do not make environmental quality a separate objective. Instead, they incorporate it into the NED objective and encourage agencies to evaluate the environmental effects of development only to the extent that they can be monetized. This approach places a premium on economic valuation of environmental costs, which in turn means that these costs will be given full weight only if agencies both have and use adequate valuation technology. However, the Guidelines do not require agencies to gain scientific understanding of affected ecosystems or to use nonmarket techniques to value those ecosystems. Thus, benefit-cost analyses conducted under the Guidelines are likely to be weakened by the limitations on science and economics discussed in the previous two chapters.

The Guidelines suggest that agencies consider all reasonable project alternatives, including the following:

- the plan that maximizes NED;
- plans that consider other federal and state concerns;
- plans requiring changes in existing statutes, regulations, administrative procedures, or common law; and
- existing state water resource plans.

However, the Guidelines recommend selection of the plan that has the greatest net national economic benefit and is consistent with protecting environmental quality. In practice, this decision criterion gives primary weight to nonenvironmental economic benefits and encourages selection of the NED plan.

The Guidelines recommend establishing four different accounts to facilitate display and evaluation of the benefits and costs of alternative project plans. The first is the NED account. The second is the environmental quality (EQ) account, which shows natural resource and environmental quality effects that are not quantified in dollar terms. The third is the regional economic development (RED) account, which shows regional economic effects such as income transfers and changes in employment. The fourth is the other social effects (OSE) account, which registers any relevant positive or negative effects not captured by the other accounts. Although the Guidelines provide that the four accounts *may* be used to show and evaluate project benefits and costs, they state that only the NED account *must* be quantified in monetary terms. The following discussion is limited to the NED and EQ accounts, which are the most important ones for purposes of this monograph.

## The National Economic Development Account

□ *Plan Benefits*. Beneficial plan effects to be monetized in the NED account include the following:

- primary effects, which include the value of any increases in national output of goods and services (or of any reductions in the costs of producing existing output levels);
- secondary effects, which include the value of external economies resulting from a plan (e.g., reduced downstream water treatment costs); and
- the value associated with use of otherwise unemployed or underemployed labor resources.

The primary benefits to be monetized include those resulting from the following market and nonmarket goods and services:

- municipal and industrial water supply;
- agricultural flooding, erosion, and sedimentation reduction;
- agricultural drainage;
- agricultural irrigation;
- urban flood damage reduction;

- transportation (inland and deepdraft navigation);
- recreation; and
- commercial fishing.

For each category, the Guidelines provide step-by-step guidance on forecasting the amount that the project would cause to be produced and used and on applying specific methodologies to quantify the resulting dollar benefits. They specify that the benefits of each alternative project plan should be valued based on users' aggregate WTP for each increment of benefit from that plan. Aggregate WTP is defined as the value that would be obtained "if the seller of the output were able to charge a variable unit price and charge each user an individual price to capture the full value of the output to the user."[18] This measure of user benefit can best be determined if the demand function for the particular good or service is known. The Guidelines state that it usually will not be possible to measure actual demand situations for project outputs and suggest four alternative techniques for estimating the values of those outputs when their demand situations are unknown.

The first technique, "actual or simulated market price," assesses the incremental benefit derived from a project's additional output of a market good or service. The technique estimates additional total revenue by multiplying expected price by expected additional quantity sold. The expected price to be used in this calculation is the existing market price if it will not be affected by the increase in output, or the midway point between the original and subsequent prices if it will.

The Guidelines suggest using the second technique, "changes in net income," to estimate the value of a project's additional output of an intermediate good that contributes to production of a market good. The technique measures changes in the net income of the producers of the market good. It is based on the theory that an increase in supply of the intermediate good lowers the cost of producing the market good, and the net benefit of the project output is the net income increase resulting from that cost reduction. Net income is calculated by multiplying the market good's price by its quantity and subtracting the market value of its inputs.

If the benefits of a project good or service cannot be estimated using market price or net income, the Guidelines recommend a third technique, "cost of the most likely alternative." If, and only if, evidence indicates that without the federal plan a nonfederal entity is likely to provide a similar output, the cost of providing this output may be used as a proxy for its value.

The fourth valuation technique uses "administratively established values," which are proxy values for specific goods and services. The Guidelines set out ad hoc unit-day proxy values for various types of recreational activities.[19]

□ *Plan Costs.* The adverse effects to be quantified in the NED account are the opportunity costs of the resources that a project plan would use. These include the following:

- implementation outlays for construction, operation and maintenance, and replacement;
- all costs related to those outlays; and
- other direct costs, defined as costs of resources which are directly required for a plan but for which no implementation outlays are made.

The third category includes the economic value of the ecological, recreational, and other goods and services that will be foregone if a plan is implemented. It might include, for example, the value of lost recreational opportunities or downstream flood damage caused by wetland drainage. If these costs can be quantified in dollar terms, they are to be included in the NED account. If not, they are to be determined in a specified alternative manner and shown in the EQ account.[20]

The Guidelines state that NED costs should be measured by WTP. When market prices reflect the full economic value of resources that would be used for development, they reflect WTP and are to be used to measure costs. Thus, market prices can serve to measure such NED costs as construction, operating, maintenance, and associated dollar expenditures. Such cost estimations are straightforward. However, market prices may not exist for some resource uses foregone with development, such as displaced recreational opportunities or ecological goods such as flood reduction services. The Guidelines suggest that it may often be impossible to calculate such costs. In contrast to their elaborate guidance on project benefits, the Guidelines do not give specific guidance on estimating project costs in the form of lost non-market environmental goods and services, except for recreational services.

□ *Flaws in NED Account.* Benefit-cost analyses conducted by the Corps and other federal water resource agencies have been heavily criticized.[21] Some of the problems cited involve the methods used to estimate future production and use of project goods and services,[22] the methodologies used to quantify dollar benefits,[23] and the discount rates used to estimate present values.[24]

This monograph focuses on another important problem: lack of attention to estimating the environmental values foregone with development. To the extent that reductions in wetland and other environmental goods and services can be identified, quantified, and appropriately monetized and included in the NED account as project costs, the Guidelines' emphasis on maximizing net NED benefits is consistent with economic efficiency. However, these costs may easily be ignored, because it is often difficult to place dollar values on nonmarket environmental goods and to predict how development may affect those goods. One partial solution to this problem is the realization that some of the procedures and methodologies set out by the Guidelines for forecasting and monetizing project benefits could also be used to estimate environmental costs.

*The Environmental Quality Account*

The Guidelines do provide procedures for evaluating environmental effects that are not quantified as NED costs. Those effects are displayed in the EQ account. The EQ process identifies and describes the beneficial and adverse effects of alternative plans on significant natural resources by evaluating the ecological, cultural, and aesthetic attributes of those resources. The ecological attributes to be considered include the following:

- functional aspects, such as ability to assimilate pollution or support commercial fisheries;
- structural aspects, such as diversity of plant and animal species and habitats; and
- chemical and physical properties of hydrology and geography.

The Guidelines specify various "indicators" to be used in evaluating expected effects on ecological attributes. Indicators are resource characteristics that can serve as direct or indirect means of describing changes in attribute quality and quantity. Federal water resource agencies are instructed to develop and apply guidelines for judging whether the environmental effects measured by the indicators are adverse or beneficial. These guidelines should include standards, criteria, or thresholds based on institutional, public, or technical recognition. For example, guidelines based on institutional recognition might include the resource attributes and measurement criteria presently recognized in laws, executive orders, regulations, and local plans and ordinances. Guidelines based on public recognition would include resource attributes and measurement criteria that the public has shown, by controversy or support, that it considers important. Guidelines based on technical recognition would reflect scientific or technical knowledge or judgment of critical resource characteristics and measurement standards.

The EQ evaluation is to proceed in four phases. The first phase defines the resources to be evaluated. This involves identifying significant resource attributes and developing a framework for measuring project plan effects on those attributes. The second phase inventories existing resource attributes and conditions and forecasts "with plan" and "without plan" future conditions. The third phase assesses the effects of alternative plans on resources and their attributes. These effects are identified, described, and evaluated for significance based on the indicator guidelines.

The last phase consists of a final appraisal of the environmental effects of alternative plans. Significant effects on resource attribute indicators are evaluated individually and collectively for each plan; they are classified as beneficial or adverse based on the evaluation guidelines and best professional judgment. The final output of the EQ evaluation should classify each alternative plan as having

- a net beneficial EQ effect,
- a net adverse EQ effect, or
- no EQ effect.

Although the Guidelines establish the EQ account for evaluation of project environmental effects, this evaluation is only qualitative and thus does not enter into the formal benefit-cost balancing. Given the Guidelines' preference for project plans that show net NED benefits, nonmonetary evaluation of environmental effects will bias benefit-cost analyses toward project justification. The potential negative impacts of Corps projects on wetlands receive greater consideration in project decisionmaking if evaluated in the NED account rather than the EQ account. Moving these impacts into the NED account means quantifying them in dollar terms.

## Political and Institutional Barriers to Economic Valuation of Wetlands

Benefit-cost analyses are critically important to decisions on prospective Corps water projects, and favorable benefit-cost ratios are prerequisites of project funding. When the Corps conducts benefit-cost analyses, it generally uses the WRC Guidelines to evaluate projects' contributions to NED. The Guidelines describe in detail how to monetize certain anticipated project benefits and costs, but they offer little assistance in evaluating and monetizing potential environmental costs. Instead, they provide environmental quality criteria that can be used to evaluate these costs *qualitatively*. They thus assume implicitly that nonmarket environmental costs are not amenable to monetization and inclusion in NED evaluations. NED analyses thus can, and often do, ignore these impacts; this is of critical concern because these analyses are the primary criteria on which most project decisions turn. In some cases, more thorough economic accounting of environmental costs would probably lead to rejection of projects that would otherwise be approved.

The fact that the Guidelines are structured this way reflects a series of political decisions to value market goods over nonmarket environmental goods. The fact that the Guidelines are implemented to maximize this preference reflects institutional agreement with it. These political and institutional barriers reinforce one another, so both political and institutional decisions would be necessary to overcome them and to ensure proper valuation of nonmarket goods such as wetland goods.

On the political side, Congress would have to amend the Guidelines to provide for monetization and adequate consideration of nonmarket goods and would have to overcome institutional resistance by making the Guidelines mandatory. Given the longstanding national preference for economic growth at the expense of environmental protection, both these political decisions could be extremely difficult.

If Congress improved the Guidelines but did not make them mandatory, implementing agencies could still ensure proper valuation of wetland goods by voluntarily following the amended Guidelines or otherwise using available techniques to assess potential environmental costs. However, the decision to properly value these costs appears less likely to be made on the institutional than on the political plane. Agencies such as the Corps perform the NED analyses for projects that they then build and operate. This potential conflict of interest, coupled with substantial latitude in the types of project impacts considered in NED analyses, suggests that even if agencies had better guidance on quantifying and monetizing environmental costs, they might not use that guidance to account more thoroughly for those costs. Moreover, even if Congress makes the Guidelines mandatory, they will only be fully effective if agencies follow them in spirit as well as to the letter.

Although the political decisions necessary for proper consideration of wetland values in water resource decisionmaking will not be easy, recent intense public concern with environmental protection should make them easier than they once were. The increasing risk that Congress will lay down strict rules mandating proper consideration of environmental costs should motivate agencies voluntarily to improve their consideration of those costs. In any case, if we are serious about ensuring efficient use of wetland resources, we should seek to overcome the inertia and implement the political and institutional changes outlined above. Chapter Five illustrates the legislative possibilities by evaluating the congressional approach to another difficult problem of resource valuation.

## Notes to Chapter 4

1. Other federal agencies are also involved in evaluating, constructing, and operating major water projects (e.g., dams, levees, canals, and reservoirs) that can adversely affect wetlands. These include the Bureau of Reclamation (Department of the Interior), the Soil Conservation Service (Department of Agriculture), and the Tennessee Valley Authority. The Corps, however, is the principal federal agency charged with evaluating, constructing, and operating major flood control and navigation projects. Most of these projects now serve multiple purposes, including irrigation, hydroelectric power generation, municipal and industrial water supply, and recreation. The Corps maintains and operates 275 major dams for flood control; 219 major lock and dam facilities for navigation; 25,000 miles of waters; over 100 commercial ports; and 416 small boat harbors. (U.S. Government Accounting Office, 1983).

2. The Corps also regulates some private activities that may affect wetlands. For example, no one may discharge dredge or fill material into navigable waters or their wetlands without obtaining a permit from the Corps. FWPCA §404, 33 U.S.C. §1344, ELR STAT. FWPCA 054. This permit program determines the fate of a significant class of wetland resources. In making permit decisions, however, the Corps qualitatively balances the expected economic benefits articulated by the permit applicant against an array of other factors, including expected wetland impacts. Since this process does not involve quantification and monetization of expected project costs and benefits, it is not discussed in this chapter.

3. Rivers and Harbors Act of 1899, 33 U.S.C. §401 (1982).

4. S. REP. No. 126, 99th Cong., 1st Sess. (1985).

5. 33 U.S.C. §2201 (Supp. V 1987).

6. Hunt, *The Need for Riparian Habitat Protection,* NAT'L WETLANDS NEWSL., Sept./Oct. 1985, at 5.

7. R. TINER, WETLANDS OF THE UNITED STATES: CURRENT STATUS AND RECENT TRENDS (U.S. Fish and Wildlife Service, U.S. Dep't of Interior, 1984).

8. *Id., see also* C. HUNT, DOWN BY THE RIVER: THE IMPACT OF FEDERAL WATER PROJECTS AND POLICIES ON BIOLOGICAL DIVERSITY (1988); *The Lower Mississippi Alluvial Plain and the Prairie Pothole Region,* in 1 THE IMPACT OF FEDERAL PROGRAMS ON WETLANDS: A REPORT TO CONGRESS BY THE SECRETARY OF THE INTERIOR (Oct. 1988).

9. *See* 33 U.S.C. §§545, 547a, 701a, 2282. If the project is inactive, this evaluation must be updated before construction may begin.

10. The Office of Management and Budget reviews the Corps' benefit-cost analyses several times during the planning process.

11. 33 U.S.C. §701(a)-(f), (h) (1982).

12. *E.g.,* B. HOLMES, HISTORY OF FEDERAL WATER RESOURCE PROGRAMS AND POLICIES (Misc. Pub. No. 1379, Economics, Statistics, and Cooperative Research Service, U.S. Dep't of Agriculture, 1979); L. JAMES & R. LEE, ECONOMICS OF WATER RESOURCES PLANNING (1971).

13. *See* B. HOLMES, *supra* note 12.

14. *Id.*

15. This task force included representatives of the Departments of Agriculture, Interior, and Defense.

16. WATER RESOURCES COUNCIL, U.S. DEP'T OF INTERIOR, ECONOMIC AND ENVIRONMENTAL PRINCIPLES AND GUIDELINES FOR WATER AND RELATED LAND RESOURCES IMPLEMENTATION STUDIES (1983).

17. The Corps' use of the WRC Guidelines is discussed in U.S. ARMY CORPS OF ENGINEERS, PAMPHLET No. 1105-2-40 (Sept. 5, 1986).

18. *See supra* pp. 22-25.

19. *See supra* pp. 36-39 for a discussion of the basis of these values.

20. *See infra* pp. 61-62.

21. *See, e.g.,* B. HOLMES, *supra* note 12; M. ZELDIN & C. BLAKENY, HOW TO COPE WITH THE CORPS (1982).

22. For example, critics contend that the Corps often estimates water supply and flood control benefits without accurately analyzing society's projected needs. It may, for instance, overstate population increases, thus boosting the future use rate estimates that underlie project benefit estimates.

23. For example, use of current market prices or arbitrary price changes to estimate future dollar benefits of project goods has been criticized.

24. Benefit-cost ratios involving streams of benefits and costs over time are extremely sensitive to the rate used to discount future values.

# Chapter 5:
# The Natural Resource Damage Assessment Regulations

T he WRC Guidelines are not the only framework that the federal government has established for valuing natural resources. For example, it has recently developed a system for assessing damages to public resources caused by releases of oil and hazardous substances. This chapter explores that system, which provides an illuminating contrast to the one established for evaluating water development impacts.

### Allocation of Public Natural Resources

Certain natural resources are owned and controlled by federal, state, and local governments. Unlike private resources, which are allocated primarily by markets, these public resources are allocated mainly by statutes and regulations designed to ensure that any allocation change benefits society. This is the underlying rationale for evaluation of the costs and benefits of federal water development proposals. In another context, Executive Order 12291 forbids major federal regulatory actions involving public natural resource modifications unless their expected societal benefits outweigh their expected costs.[1] This order governs most federal regulations on natural resource use.

The courts also play an important role in allocating public resources by providing a forum for correcting infringements of allocation rights. For example, if an oil spill injures public resources, thus diminishing the quantity or quality of goods and services provided to society, government trustees of the resources must look to the courts for compensation.

As the previous chapters have argued in the water development context, agencies and courts can allocate public natural resources efficiently only if they can accurately value modifications and injuries to those resources. Such valuation is necessary in order to compare an environment's original economic productivity, or total contribution to social welfare, with its productivity after a modification or injury. Statutory, regulatory, and judicial mechanisms for valuation of public resource injuries have varied widely in accuracy, however. While monetary evaluation of the environmental effects of water resource development has been seriously lacking, such evaluation has been conducted far more frequently and effectively in other contexts. Some of the latest regulatory approaches are fairly accurate and sophisticated. For example, federal regulatory impact analyses increasingly evaluate the social benefits of regulatory options based on economic measures of welfare change. Moreover, regulators increasingly use nonmarket valuation techniques to assess the value of natural resources that are not traded in organized markets.

While certain federal agencies have become more sophisticated and accurate in valuing natural resources, courts have generally lagged behind. Under common law, courts correctly seek to determine the amount of monetary compensation that will make the public "whole," or as well off after a natural resource injury as before. This measure of damages represents the social value of the resource injury. It both sets the correct amount of compensation and gives potential polluters the appropriate level of incentive to limit resource injuries. However, courts have historically based this measure of damages on diminution of market prices. Since these prices do not directly indicate net benefits, price changes are not economically correct measures of welfare change. Moreover, with some notable exceptions,[2] nonmarket valuation techniques have not yet played a substantial role in litigation. Courts have generally derived damages to injured nonmarket resources exclusively on the basis of the costs of restoring or replacing those resources.

The Comprehensive Environmental Response, Compensation, and Liability Act (CERCLA)[3] could lead to improvements in both regulatory and judicial valuation of natural resource damages.[4] CERCLA relies on agencies to calculate these damages and on courts to enforce them; agency assessments enjoy a presumption of accuracy in enforcement actions. The statute encourages agencies to apply nonmarket valuation techniques to resource damages and opens the door for courts to do the same. It is thus an important step toward regulatory and judicial use of economically appropriate and accurate nonmarket valuation methods. While CERCLA's framework is still very new and has yet to be tested in the field, it holds much promise. Eventually, it is likely to set the rules for using economic analysis in a wide range of judicial proceedings involving injured natural resources. In many ways, it could also become a model for wetland valuation in the context of water resource development.

## CERCLA Natural Resource Damage Assessment Provisions

CERCLA forces hazardous substance generators, handlers, and disposers to internalize the social costs of their polluting activities. Pursuant to CERCLA and §311 of the FWPCA,[5] governmental trustees may recover damages for the public natural resource injuries caused by oil discharges or hazardous substance releases. This reflects congressional recognition that hazardous substance contamination may impose social costs that would not be fully redressed by site cleanups or private actions under state common law. Other federal statutes also provide for recovery of natural resource damages.[6] CERCLA, however, goes far beyond these other laws by defining compensable damages broadly and by establishing a regulatory structure to guide their assessment.

CERCLA defines natural resources very broadly to include land, fish, wildlife, biota, air, water, groundwater, drinking water supplies, and other such resources.[7] It defines compensable injury as "injury to, destruction of, or loss of natural resources, including the reasonable costs of assessing such injury, loss or destruction."[8] Liability for such injury "shall be to the U.S. government and to any State for natural resources within the State or belonging to, managed by, controlled by, or appertaining to such State," and "the President, or authorized representative of any State, shall act on behalf of the public as trustee of such natural resources, to recover for such damages."[9] Courts have held that under certain circumstances, local governments may also qualify as natural resource trustees and may sue for natural resource damages pursuant to CERCLA and the FWPCA.[10] CERCLA specifies that funds recovered by natural resource trustees in such actions can be used only to "restore, replace, or acquire the equivalent of . . . natural resources . . . . The measure of damages in any action . . . shall not be limited by the sums which can be used to restore or replace such resources."[11]

Besides establishing a structure for suing for damages to public resources, CERCLA creates a formal regulatory system for estimating those damages. The statute provides for development of natural resource damage assessment guidelines to assist governmental trustees in bringing claims. It directs the President to promulgate regulations

containing two types of standardized guidelines: Type A procedures
for cases involving small releases and Type B protocols for cases involving major releases. Type A procedures are "standardized procedures for simplified assessments requiring minimal field observation, including establishing measures of damages based on units of
discharge or release units or units of affected area."[12] Type B protocols are "alternative protocols for conducting assessments in individual cases to determine the type and extent of short- and long-
term injury, destruction, or loss."[13] The regulations "shall identify
the best available procedures to determine such damages, including
both direct and indirect injury, destruction, or loss and shall take into consideration factors including, but not limited to, replacement
value, use value, and ability of the ecosystem or resource to recover."[14]
The inclusion of use value as a damage assessment factor indicates
congressional recognition that equitable and efficient natural resource
damage determinations often require economic-based measures of
welfare change.

Damage assessments conducted according to these guidelines enjoy
a "rebuttable presumption" of accuracy in any administrative or ad-
judicatory proceeding by the trustee under CERCLA or FWPCA
§311.[15] The presumption gives trustees who follow the regulations
leverage in proving damage claims, but the exact nature and extent
of this leverage are unclear.[16]

President Reagan directed the Department of the Interior (DOI)
to promulgate the damage assessment regulations.[17] The final Type
B and Type A regulations were promulgated on August 1, 1986[18] and
March 20, 1987,[19] respectively. In 1986, the Superfund Amendments
and Reauthorization Act (SARA) added more damage assessment provisions and directed the President to amend the regulations to incorporate them. Amended Type A and B regulations were issued on
February 22, 1988.[20] As a result of a petition filed by several states
and environmental groups, the U.S. Court of Appeals for the District
of Columbia Circuit remanded certain provisions of the regulations
to DOI in July 1989.[21] The following discussion summarizes the regulations and the consequences of the partial remand.

## Type A Regulations

Type A regulations have been developed to calculate damages for
wildlife mortality and for closure of recreational areas resulting from
discharges or releases that affect coastal or marine environments near

the water surface or intertidal area for a short period of time.[22] A computer model calculates these damages given data on the type of discharge or release and the specific receiving environment. The model is capable of calculating the following types of resource damages: short-term lethal effects on lower trophic biota; direct and indirect lethal effects on fur seals, certain waterfowl and other shorebirds, seabirds, fish, and shellfish; and closure of fishing areas, hunting areas, and public beaches.

The model employs three interactive submodels and data bases:

- a physical fates submodel that determines average contaminant concentration, transportation, and dispersion, using a chemical data base;
- a biological effects submodel that calculates average biomass loss by species category, given information from the physical fates submodel and a biological data base; and
- an economic submodel that values resource damages, given information from the biological effects submodel and an economic data base that provides values for resource services.

For some services, including commercial use of fur seals, commercial and recreational fishing, hunting, birdwatching, and public beach use, the economic data base provides dollar values. For example, it includes the market value and the costs of commercial fish landings, thus allowing calculation of the dollar value of landings foregone. For other services, the data base provides nonmarket values based on unit WTP estimates derived from existing studies.

Although the Type A model includes WTP-based unit measures of resource use value, it has several important limitations. It applies only to short-term discharges to or near marine or coastal water surfaces or intertidal areas. It does not ascertain damages resulting from sublethal and chronic low-level effects or damages for mortality to many wildlife species. Also, the values in the economic data base cannot be used to calculate resource damages if a discharge can be expected to significantly change recreational or commercial prices for the damaged resources. These constraints severely limit the model's potential applicability to the wide range of discharges and releases covered by CERCLA. The Type A regulations therefore specify that if a trustee has reason to believe that the types of potential resource injuries are different from those covered by the model, or if any other model condition or assumption is violated, the Type B procedures should be used instead.

The D.C. Circuit has remanded the Type A rules to DOI. The court emphasized that the rules improperly rely exclusively on lost use values, ignoring restoration and replacement values.[23] This rationale is explored further in the following sections.

## Type B Regulations

The Type B regulations set out the guidelines trustees are to use for estimating resource damages when the Type A model does not apply. They set out basic procedures, methodologies, and criteria for:

- determining the natural resource injuries resulting from oil or hazardous substance releases under CERCLA and FWPCA §301;
- quantifying the effects of those injuries on human uses of resource services; and
- valuing reductions in those uses (i.e., determining natural resource damages).

The last step explicitly recognizes and authorizes use of the more sophisticated economic techniques for estimating nonmarket resource values. Technical Information Documents that accompany the regulations give more detailed guidance on using specified injury quantification and damage valuation methodologies.

CERCLA allows trustees to recover only the "reasonable" costs of damage assessments, and the Type B regulations reflect this limitation. Assessment costs are deemed reasonable when

(1) the injury, quantification, and damages determination phases have a well-defined relationship to one another and are coordinated;

(2) the anticipated increment of extra benefits, in terms of the precision or accuracy of estimates, obtained by using a more costly methodology for injury quantification or damage determination outweigh the anticipated increment of extra costs of the more expensive procedure; and

(3) the anticipated costs of performing the assessment are expected to be less than the anticipated damage amount.[24]

Three regulatory subparts contain guidelines for performing damage assessments. Subpart B provides for a "pre-assessment screen," which determines whether an assessment is warranted based on a "desk top" review of existing data and evidence.

Subpart C requires development of a comprehensive "Assessment Plan," which identifies and documents all the scientific and economic procedures and methodologies to be used in assessing and valuing resource injuries. The documentation must be detailed enough to facilitate determination of whether the proposed approaches are "cost-effective." Cost-effective means that "when two or more activities provide the same or a similar level of benefits, the least cost activity providing that level of benefits will be selected."[25] In other words, each specific procedure or methodology to be used in assessing damages must be capable of achieving the desired results at the lowest possible cost.

Because the alternative valuation techniques allowed by CERCLA will yield different estimates of resource value, the Assessment Plan must pay special attention to identifying and documenting the economic methodologies to be used. Following the statute, the regulations set out an Economic Methodology Determination that allows damage calculations to be based either on restoration or replacement costs or on diminution in use values. However, in choosing between these measures, "the authorized official shall select the lesser of: restoration or replacement costs; or diminution of use values as the measure of damages."[26] To follow this decision rule, the official should calculate rough approximations of the costs and benefits of the two measures. Costs are defined as "the expected present value, if possible, of anticipated restoration or replacement costs, expressed in constant dollars, and separated into capital, operating, and maintenance costs, and including the timing of the costs." Benefits are defined as "the expected present value, if possible, of anticipated use values gained through restoration or replacement, expressed in constant dollars, specified for the same base year as the cost estimate, and separated into recurring or nonrecurring benefits, including the timing of the benefit."[27]

The "lesser of restoration cost or use value" provision reflects DOI's determination that such a decision rule is necessary to ensure economically efficient damage awards. This argues that if restoration cost exceeds estimated use values, it would be inefficient to award restoration costs when a lesser award based on use value would fully compensate the public.

The D.C. Circuit focused primarily on the "lesser of" rule in remanding the Type B and Type A rules to DOI. The court agreed that the rule could ensure economically efficient damages awards, but only if economic techniques were advanced enough to ensure that all lost or diminished use values would be appropriately identified and measured. The court ruled that Congress apparently rejected this assumption and created a presumption in favor of restoration costs as a measure of damages to ensure that the public would be fully compensated. Although DOI is permitted to establish some conditions under which damages can be based exclusively on lost use value— when restoration is infeasible, for example, or restoration costs grossly exceed use values—it cannot use a cost comparison alone to determine when to deviate from Congress' preference.[28]

Subpart E provides guidance for actual implementation of Assessment Plans. It outlines the procedural steps and criteria that trustees must follow in choosing and implementing methodologies for each assessment phase: injury determination, service reduction quantification, and damage valuation.

The Subpart E rules lay out a complex set of procedures, methodologies, and criteria for injury determination. Most notably, the rules require findings of resource injury to be based on *measurable* impacts on resources. These impacts must be traceable to illegal oil or hazardous substance discharges covered by CERCLA. For example, a finding of injury to biota must be based on measurable biological impacts clearly shown to be related to specific pollutants. Thus, damages can be assessed for a decrease in use of resource services resulting from sublethal or low-level chronic impacts only if the impacts are measurable and are quantitatively linked to illegal oil or hazardous substance discharges.[29]

Once a finding of resource injury is made, the rules governing quantification spell out procedures, methodologies, and criteria for quantifying the injury and the resulting reduction in resource services. This reduction forms the basis for damage calculations.[30]

The Subpart E rules on the final phase of damage assessment explicitly recognize economic techniques for ascertaining resource damages and provide guidance and criteria for appropriate use of those techniques.[31] For example, the criteria on replacement or restoration costs require use of the least-cost feasible replacement or restoration scheme that returns an injured resource's goods and services to their pre-injury condition. Damages calculated using these costs may include any diminution in use value while the resource is returning to that condition.[32]

Subpart E also establishes criteria for selecting and implementing methodologies for calculating use value. 'Use value" is defined as "the value to the public of recreational or other public uses of the resource, as measured by changes in consumer surplus, any fees or other payments collectable by the government for a private party's use of the natural resource, and any economic rent accruing to a private party because the government does not charge a fee or price for use of the resource."[33] In addition, "where the Federal or state agency acting as a trustee is the majority operator or controller of a for- or not-for-profit enterprise, and the injury to the natural resource results in a loss to such an enterprise, that portion of the lost income from this enterprise . . . may be included as a measure of damages."[34] Damages may be based on diminished use value for only as long as it takes the resource to recover naturally.[35]

This definition of "use value" expresses a much more sophisticated concept of natural resource value than has often been used in the past. However, while the regulations provide for WTP-based measures of resource damages, they limit the application of these measures in certain important respects. For example, they allow damages to be based on diminished use value only for "committed uses" of resources. A committed use is a current or planned public use of a natural resource for which there is a documented legal, administrative, budgetary, or financial commitment before the oil discharge or hazardous substance release is detected.[36] In addition, "baseline uses must be reasonably probable, not just in the realm of possibility. Purely speculative uses of the injured resource are precluded from consideration in the estimation of damages."[37]

Subpart E sets out the specific methodologies that trustees may use to estimate lost use value and provides guidance for selecting among them. This guidance applies one group of valuation methodologies to market resources and another to nonmarket resources, and prescribes a hierarchy among the methodologies in each group.

When an injured resource is traded in a reasonably competitive market, its trustee must first turn to the market price methodology, which simply calculates damages as the difference in the resource's market price before and after the injury. If a trustee determines that this methodology is not applicable to a particular resource, he or she should next investigate the appraisal methodology, which calculates damages as the reduction in the resource's appraisal value. Trustees are instructed to turn to the "Uniform Appraisal Standards for Federal Land Acquisitions" for guidance in making appraisals.[38]

The D.C. Circuit has held this regulatory preference for basing natural resource damages on market prices invalid. The court held that it is reasonable to consider market price in determining use value; however, it is not reasonable to treat price as the only or predominant factor, because markets do not capture all resource values. The court instructed DOI to consider allowing trustees to define use values as the sum of all reliably calculated use values, however measured, and excluding double counting.[39]

The rules provide that when trustees value nonmarket resources to which the market-oriented methodologies are not applicable, they may use any nonmarket valuation methodology that estimates use values based on WTP. The regulations explicitly discuss some of the available techniques.[40] For example, they authorize use of the NFI method to estimate damages to resources that serve as inputs into market goods. They authorize use of the TC, hedonic pricing, and CV methods to estimate damages to resources that contribute directly to consumer satisfaction.[41] Finally, they authorize use of regional unit values derived from existing studies if these values are based on WTP and on resource services closely resembling those to which they are applied.

The regulations place certain restrictions on use of the CV technique for estimating damages based on nonuse (option and existence) values. They explain that the CV technique "can determine use values and explicitly determine option and existence values," but provide that "the use of the CV methodology to explicitly determine option and existence values should be used only if the authorized official determines that no other use values can be determined."[42] The preamble to the rules acknowledges that option and existence values would ordinarily be additive to use values but notes that CERCLA §301(c) only mentions use values, not nonuse values.

These restrictions have been invalidated by the D.C. Circuit. The court held that CERCLA §301(c)(2) is not limited to use values, and that even if it were, DOI has not explained why it does not recognize option and existence values as compensable values, given that they represent utility derived from resources.[43]

The regulations also provide guidance on various issues related to implementation of valuation methodologies, including possible double-counting problems, uncertainty in damages determinations, and discounting of costs and benefits over time (the rules mandate a 10 percent discount rate).[44] A Technical Information Document accompanying the regulations provides additional detailed guidance on applying the various techniques.[45]

## Assessment of CERCLA Framework and Comparison With WRC Guidelines

The CERCLA natural resource damage framework has standardized the criteria, procedures, and methodologies used for assessing and recovering damages for public natural resource injuries resulting from hazardous waste releases. Perhaps most importantly, the federal rules have introduced newer and economically more accurate WTP-based nonmarket valuation methods for assessing natural resource damages. Increased reliance on these methods should result in more equitable compensation for natural resource injuries as well as more appropriate prospective incentives to limit those injuries.

While the regulations as they stand expand the potential for use of nonmarket valuation techniques, they simultaneously limit the broader application of those techniques in several ways.[46] The most important limitation is the hierarchy of methods for measuring lost use values. The D.C. Circuit correctly struck down this hierarchy, which limits the use of appropriate economic techniques in two important respects.

First, the hierarchy gives precedence to the use of diminution in market price or appraisal value as a measure of recovery. This is likely to result in undervaluation of resource injury, because market prices do not directly indicate the net benefits provided by market goods in general or public natural resources in particular. For example, under the rules, the entrance fee charged for access to a national park could serve as the measure of damages for injury to the park. As the D.C. Circuit noted: "This is quite obviously and totally fallacious; there is no necessary connection between the total value to the public of a park and the fees charged as admission which typically are set not to maximize profits but rather to encourage the public to visit the park."[47] The court correctly held that it is reasonable to look to market prices as one factor, but not the exclusive or predominant factor, in determining resource use value.

Second, the hierarchy disallows measurement of nonuse values, such as option and existence values, unless no direct use values can be estimated. The D.C. Circuit correctly concluded that the benefits provided by public resources include both direct use values and any nonuse values that may exist. Accordingly, the court instructed DOI to rewrite the rules to include nonuse values.[48]

The D.C. Circuit's rulings on these provisions, as well as on those restricting use of the CV methodology, will foster more appropriate use of economic techniques for measuring natural resource damages and will eliminate some important barriers that the current regulations place in the way of appropriate measurement of natural resource value. On the other hand, the court struck down the "lesser of restoration costs or use value" provision, which would have fostered greater reliance on nonmarket valuation methods.

Despite forthcoming changes in the rules to reflect the preference for restoration costs as the measure of resource damages, the CERCLA damage assessment system has greater potential for fostering the use and further development of nonmarket valuation techniques than does the WRC evaluation system. In certain resource damage cases, for example, the presumption for restoration cost will fall away in favor of methods for measuring use values. Even when restoration cost is used to measure damages, nonmarket valuation methods will often be needed to measure lost use values during the time required for complete restoration. Thus, unlike the water development context, in which nonmarket valuation techniques have been little used, few cases are likely to be brought under the natural resource damages assessment framework that will not rely to some extent on these methods.

Comparison of the CERCLA and WRC frameworks also highlights institutional problems with the WRC framework. Legislative and institutional politics have created at least three major differences between the two frameworks. First, natural resource trustees must use the economic approaches in the CERCLA regulations to benefit from the rebuttable presumption that their assessments are accurate. Agencies seeking this presumption *must* use specified procedures and techniques in order to seek natural resource damages and *must* follow specified criteria in determining when to apply nonmarket valuation techniques. In contrast, the economic approaches in the WRC Guidelines are merely advisory. Agencies are not required to use the Guidelines in evaluating proposed water projects, and are not bound by specific criteria in deciding whether to use nonmarket valuation techniques. They are not even required to explicitly incorporate impacts on nonmarket resources into their benefit-cost analyses. Their failure to follow the Guidelines incurs no consequences. Any regulatory program that seeks to improve economic analysis will be more effective if it mandates—or at least rewards—the improvements rather than merely suggests them.

Second, the CERCLA regulations are more comprehensive than the WRC Guidelines. The regulations and the Guidelines discuss many of the same nonmarket valuation techniques, including the NFI, CV, and TC techniques. However, although the CERCLA regulations include criteria for deciding when to apply these methodologies, the Guidelines do not. Inclusion of these criteria facilitates use of nonmarket techniques for assessing CERCLA natural resource damages. Their exclusion discourages use of those techniques for assessing wetland damages resulting from water projects.

Third, agency analyses under the CERCLA regulations are subject to independent review; those under the Guidelines are not. CERCLA provides for judicial review of agency damage assessments. An assessment that does not follow the regulations loses its presumption of accuracy. In contrast, benefit-cost analyses used to evaluate water projects are not subject to independent review for completeness and accuracy. The agencies that conduct the analyses also construct and operate the projects. Moreover, federal courts generally have declined to review the adequacy of agency analyses at the request of public interest groups.[49] Agencies' proprietary interest in seeing projects approved, coupled with lack of independent review, has led to incomplete and often erroneous use of economics in benefit-cost analyses.

The following chapter presents recommendations for improving the economic valuation of water project impacts on wetlands and for incorporating that valuation into project decisions. Some of these recommendations are based on lessons learned from the CERCLA natural resource damage assessment framework.

## Notes to Chapter 5

1. Exec. Order No. 12291, 3 C.F.R. 127 (1982), *reprinted in* ELR Admin. Mat. 45025.

2. For example, nonmarket valuation techniques were used to assess some of the damage claims resulting from the 1978 *Amoco Cadiz* oil spill off the Brittany coast.

3. 42 U.S.C. §§9601-9675, ELR Stat. 44001-81. CERCLA, as strengthened and extended by the Superfund Amendments and Reauthorization Act of 1986 (SARA), was enacted primarily to deal with the threats posed by abandoned hazardous waste sites and hazardous substance releases. It gives federal and state governments broad authorities to clean up waste sites and otherwise respond to releases of hazardous substances into the environment. CERCLA also provides mechanisms for the government to recover its response costs from parties responsible for such releases. Current and former owners and operators of polluting vessels or facilities, as well as those who generate, treat, or dispose of hazardous substances, are liable for damages resulting from releases.

4. Natural resource damage provisions are set out in CERCLA §§107, 111, & 301; 42 U.S.C. §§9607, 9611 & 9651, ELR Stat. 44024, 44034 & 44067.

5. FWPCA §311, 33 U.S.C. §1321, ELR Stat. FWPCA 039.

6. *See, e.g.,* Trans-Alaska Pipeline Authorization Act, 43 U.S.C. §1653(a)(1), (c)(1); Deepwater Port Act, 33 U.S.C. §1517(d); Outer Continental Shelf Lands Act Amendments of 1978, 43 U.S.C. §1813(b)(3).

7. CERCLA §101(16), 42 U.S.C. §9601(16), ELR Stat. 44006.

8. CERCLA §107(a)(4)(C), 42 U.S.C. §9607(a)(4)(C), ELR Stat. 44024.

9. CERCLA §107(f)(1), 42 U.S.C. §9607(f)(1), ELR Stat. 44026.

10. *See* Maraziti, *Local Governments: Opportunities to Recover for Natural Resource Damages,* 17 ELR 10036 (1987).

11. CERCLA §107(f)(1), 42 U.S.C. §9607(f)(1), ELR Stat. 44026. This provision has been held to mean that damages exceeding restoration or replacement costs must be spent on acquiring the equivalent of the injured resource, in compensation for the use value that is lost while restoration or replacement is in progress. Ohio v. Department of the Interior, No. 86-1529, slip op. at 44-46 (D.C. Cir. July 14, 1989).

12. CERCLA §301(c)(2), 42 U.S.C. §9651(c)(2), ELR Stat. 44067.

13. *Id.*

14. *Id.*

15. CERCLA §107(f)(2)(C), 42 U.S.C. §9607(f)(2)(C), ELR Stat. 44026; FWPCA §311, 33 U.S.C. §1321, ELR Stat. FWPCA 039.

16. For a discussion of the meaning and potential force and effect of the presumption, see Menefee, *Recovery for Natural Resource Damages Under Superfund: The Role of the Rebuttable Presumption,* 12 ELR 15057 (1982).

17. Exec. Order No. 12316, 3 C.F.R. 168 (1981), *rescinded by* Exec. Order No. 12580, 3 C.F.R. 193 (1987), *reprinted in* ELR ADMIN. MAT. 45031.

18. 43 C.F.R. pt. 11, 51 Fed. Reg. 27674 (Aug. 1, 1986).

19. 43 C.F.R. pt. 11, 52 Fed. Reg. 9042 (Mar. 20, 1987).

20. 53 Fed. Reg. 5166 (Feb. 22, 1988).

21. Ohio v. Department of the Interior, No. 86-1529 (D.C. Cir. July 14, 1989); Colorado v. Department of the Interior, No. 87-1265 (D.C. Cir. July 14, 1989).

22. 43 C.F.R. pt. 11.

23. Colorado v. Department of the Interior, No. 87-1265, slip op. at 19-20 (D.C. Cir. July 14, 1989).

24. 43 C.F.R. §11.14(ee). The D.C. Circuit has upheld this regulation. Ohio v. Department of the Interior, No. 86-1529, slip op. at 75-76 (D.C. Cir. July 14, 1989).

25. 43 C.F.R. §11.14(j).

26. 43 C.F.R. §11.35(b)(2).

27. 43 C.F.R. §11.35(e)(3)(i), (ii).

28. Ohio v. Department of the Interior, No. 86-1529, slip op. at 21-23, 47, 49-53 (D.C. Cir. July 14, 1989).

29. 43 C.F.R. §§11.61-.69.

30. 43 C.F.R. §§11.70-.79.

31. 43 C.F.R. §§11.80-.84.

32. 43 C.F.R. §11.81(a)-(f).

33. 43 C.F.R. §11.83(b)(1).

34. 43 C.F.R. §11.83(b)(2).

35. 43 C.F.R. §§11.83-.84.

36. 43 C.F.R. §11.14(h).

37. 43 C.F.R. §11.84(b)(2). The D.C. Circuit has upheld the "committed use" limitation. Because a trustee may recover restoration costs even when a resource has no "committed use," the limitation applies only to the calculation of lost use value prior to completion of restoration or replacement. Ohio v. Department of the Interior, No. 86-1529, slip op. at 61-63 (D.C. Cir. July 14, 1989).

38. 43 C.F.R. §11.83(c)(2).

39. Ohio v. Department of the Interior, No. 86-1529, slip op. at 63-66 (D.C. Cir. July 14, 1989).

40. 43 C.F.R. §11.83. These techniques are discussed in Chapter 3.

41. The D.C. Circuit has upheld the inclusion of CV in the regulations. Ohio v. Department of the Interior, No. 86-1529, slip op. at 92-104 (D.C. Cir. July 14, 1989).

42. 43 C.F.R. §11.83(d)(5).

43. Ohio v. Department of the Interior, No. 86-1529, slip op. at 66-67 (D.C. Cir. July 14, 1989).

44. 43 C.F.R. §11.84(e).

45. Desvousges, Type B Technical Information Document: Techniques to Measure Damages to Natural Resources (draft report prepared for CERCLA 301 Project, U.S. Dep't of Interior, Sept. 1985).

46. For a detailed discussion of this issue, see Dower & Scodari, *Compensation for Natural Resource Injury: An Emerging Federal Framework, 4* MARINE RESOURCE ECON. 155 (1987).

47. Ohio v. Department of the Interior, No. 86-1529, slip op. at 65 (D.C. Cir. July 14, 1989).

48. *Id.* at 66-67.

49. B. WEISBROD *et al.*, PUBLIC INTEREST LAW: AN ECONOMIC AND INSTITUTIONAL ANALYSIS 195-215 (1978).

# Chapter 6:
# Conclusions and
# Recommendations

This monograph has outlined some of the economic, scientific, and political parameters of wetland value assessments in the context of water resource development decisionmaking. The degree to which these assessments use nonmarket economic valuation techniques substantially affects the efficiency of project development, management, and oversight. Nonmarket techniques for valuing many wetland benefits are currently available, and the existing federal administrative framework allows decisionmakers to use them. Still, the potential for more accurate estimates of the environmental costs of development has been limited by the economic, scientific, and political factors previously described. This chapter recommends some ways to address these limitations and further the effective use of economics in federal water resource decisionmaking.

As a preliminary matter, we must recognize that Congress has significant power in this area. It is often assumed that science and economics are beyond political control and therefore that these disciplines cannot be more effectively used to protect resources until their technologies develop or data bases expand at their own pace. This is not necessarily true. For example, Congress could help reduce many of the economic limitations inherent in the current WRC Guidelines. When Congress enacted the CERCLA natural resource damage provisions, it showed that it could effectively change the rules governing the economic analysis of a set of environmental problems by recognizing, requiring the use of, and thus encouraging further development of state-of-the-art economic techniques. Congress is just as capable of changing the rules governing the economic valuation of wetlands by forcing the use and development of advanced economic technology. Congress engaged in such economic technology-forcing regarding wetlands when it proposed benefit-cost analysis in the Flood Control Act of 1936. Although the basic benefit-cost requirement is still in effect, the Guidelines implementing it do not make rigorous demands on economic technology. Indeed, the Guidelines have regressed in this regard: they encouraged economic progress for some time, then were rolled back for political reasons. Congress could change this situation if it chose. Environmentalists seeking tools for protecting wetlands thus could usefully encourage Congress to sharpen the economic tools that already exist.

The recommendations below are not limited to the field of economics. As discussed earlier, many wetland valuation difficulties stem not from failures of economics, but from failures of science or institutional mechanisms. Although we should certainly continue to refine existing economic techniques, we do not need radically new economics to value many types of wetland outputs. We do need significantly better science and considerable reform of the administrative framework.

## Methodological Improvements

### Improvement of Biological and Ecological Data Bases

No economics, however sophisticated, can determine wetland values without scientific understanding and quantification of wetland functions and their sensitivity to development. Scientific data and models quantifying the ecological relationships among wetland characteristics and outputs are the raw material for economic analyses of wetland impacts. Although wetland science has come very far in the last 20 years, we still cannot quantify wetland functions accurately enough to estimate their contributions to the production of services or the potential effects of development on the nature and supply of those services. Work in this area is ongoing at the federal level. However, the few methodologies developed for assessing and quantifying wetland functions and service flows[1] have proved too complex and cumbersome for easy, widespread application to water resource decisions.

☐ *Research.* Our major recommendation in this area is for federally sponsored research, possibly conducted or coordinated by EPA, on assessment of wetland functions and their potential responses to development. The research program should look at wetland regions, thus avoiding the need to reach consistent conclusions regarding vastly different types of wetlands yet not focusing too narrowly on individual wetlands. The program should first develop methodologies for assessing wetland functions and apply those methodologies to determine the important functions of regional wetland ecosystems. Next, it should investigate the potential cumulative effects of water resource development activities on the functions underlying production of regional wetland goods. These efforts will generate important information on the ways that cumulative water resource development might affect the supply of those goods.

☐ *Technology-forcing.* Environmentalists who perceive scientific technology as developing too slowly for effective wetlands protection should consider urging Congress to make it develop faster. Congress could, for example, establish presumptions that wetlands serve specified important functions, that these functions have specified high values, and that particular types of water resource development will diminish those values to specified significant degrees. A federal agency seeking to overcome these presumptions against development would have to furnish scientific proof that they overvalued a specific wetland or wetland region. This would encourage agencies to sponsor research into actual wetland functions and values.

### Improvement of Economic Data Bases

If we develop the scientific data and administrative structure necessary for accurate wetland valuation, we should also polish our economic valuation techniques. Currently, even sophisticated, site-specific economic assessments cannot quantify all wetland values, and the costs and expertise required for such assessments limit their use. We therefore recommend additional privately sponsored research on the theory of wetland valuation and the application of valuation methodologies. We also recommend one incremental change in the use of economics to value wetlands: the development of recreation demand analyses.

Because they are based on user behavior, economic techniques can often be used to estimate wetland values without explicit knowledge regarding the physical production of wetland goods. If the existing uses of a wetland are known, its value can be estimated. The effect of a proposed alteration on that value, however, can only be estimated if an analyst can predict how users will respond to the alteration. To do this, the analyst must tie the use to measures of the good's quality and quantity. This is done through models linking information on producer and consumer uses of wetland outputs to indices of output quality and quantity.

As a first step toward developing these models, federal resource agencies should conduct a series of regional demand analyses relating changes in demand for wetland-supported recreation to various recreational quality and quantity variables. Similar analyses have been used to estimate changes in national demand for freshwater recreational fishing in response to water quality changes resulting from the FWPCA.[2] If the relationships of the nature and supply of wetland goods to the recreational value of certain regional wetland ecosystems could be identified, they might be generalized to other such ecosystems. Of course, these studies would not provide all the data needed to predict changes in wetland recreational values; for example, it would still be necessary to determine how particular developments would alter wetlands. However, understanding the demand changes resulting from potential alterations would furnish a critical input into the predictive process.

## Improvement of Communication Among Wetland Scientists, Economists, and Decisionmakers

A project's likely impacts on a wetland can be valued only if they are known. That knowledge is primarily the purview of wetland scientists and ecologists, but it contributes to economic valuation only if it is closely tied to the kinds of variables that economists include in models of user behavior. If this connection is made, science and economics can work together to assess and protect wetlands; if not, both disciplines are less effective. Cooperation among professional disciplines is thus crucial to effective use of scientific and economic expertise to value wetland goods. This interdisciplinary cooperation should include agency decisionmakers as well as independent scientists and economists. The decisionmakers need access to state-of-the-art scientific and economic information, and the scientists and economists need to understand the context in which their contributions will be used.

This kind of joint effort has been lacking. Few institutional arrangements facilitate interaction among scientists, economists, and decisionmakers. As a result, there has been little sharing of information on wetland functions or of ideas on using this information in bioeconomic models describing the production and use of wetland goods.

We recommend that avenues be developed for cooperative research and interdisciplinary information transfer. These avenues should improve communication among wetland scientists, economists, and decisionmakers, enabling them to share data and understand one another's perspectives. As a starting point, we recommend formation of an ongoing dialogue group modeled after the Keystone Center and including a core of scientists and economists working on wetland issues.[3] The group would focus on formulating potential programs to address the issues discussed in this monograph. These programs might include joint research projects, steps to disseminate existing studies more widely, and regional interdisciplinary seminars.

In preparation for formation of the dialogue group, we recommend an interdisciplinary conference along the same lines. A private nonprofit organization could usefully sponsor such a conference, which would explore the issues in this monograph and the potential uses of a more permanent forum.

In addition, we recommend that federal agencies sponsor joint research projects, workshops, and other information transfer mechanisms.

## Legislative and Administrative Reforms: Amendments to WRC Guidelines

We recommend that the WRC Guidelines be rewritten to account more completely for the social costs of water projects. The Guidelines currently set out detailed procedures and methods for forecasting and valuing expected project benefits but not expected effects on wetland goods (except recreational goods). In contrast, the CERCLA natural resource damage regulations encourage use of nonmarket valuation techniques for valuing nonmarket resource goods. Although the hazardous waste contamination and water resource development situations differ in many ways, the CERCLA regulations suggest two initial changes that should be made to the Guidelines. First, the Guidelines should describe the economic valuation techniques applicable to nonmarket resources. Second, they should mandate application of those techniques to those resources. These changes should be mandated by Congress and implemented by the WRC.

### Guidance on Economic Techniques

The NED evaluation procedures should be amended to include detailed guidance on identifying, quantifying, and monetizing environmental outputs that projects could potentially diminish or eliminate. Most environmental effects are likely to be nonmarket impacts that can only be monetized using special techniques. However, the Guidelines already discuss many of these techniques, including NFI, TC, and CV, in the context of assessing project benefits. It should therefore be relatively easy to provide additional guidance on using these techniques to estimate the value of environmental goods and services potentially at risk.

## Mandatory Use of Economic Techniques

Even if the Guidelines provide guidance on state-of-the-art economic techniques, agencies may be institutionally reluctant to use them. Their use should therefore be mandatory. Under one possible approach, the Guidelines could require agencies to conduct preliminary investigations of the environmental benefits potentially at risk from proposed water projects, using readily available data. If such a preliminary screen indicated that these benefits might be significant, the agency would have to use available techniques to quantify and monetize them. This requirement would need to be flexible enough not to require needless analyses, but firm enough to ensure equal consideration of environmental costs and project benefits. Alternatively, the Guidelines could require use of nonmarket valuation methodologies whenever an environmental impact statement identified potential adverse impacts on wetland goods. Under either approach, agency decisions should be subject to review by an independent body to guard against potential bias.

## Conclusion

Expressing the value of a living ecosystem in economic terms is always difficult. Although recent developments in science and economics have made the task somewhat easier, truly accurate valuation will require further developments in both. Moreover, we need to restructure our institutional frameworks to incorporate the scientific and economic understanding we have already achieved. This monograph presents an overview of this complex problem and outlines recommendations that will increase the accuracy of wetlands valuation in the context of water resource development. Perhaps most importantly, however, it suggests to other researchers the numerous avenues that remain to be explored in future work.

## Notes to Chapter 6

1. 1 P. Adamus & L. Stockwell, *A Method for Wetland Functional Assessment: Critical Review and Evaluation Concepts* (Report No. FHWA-IP-82-23, Federal Highway Administration, U.S. Dep't of Transportation, Mar. 1983).

2. W. Vaughan & C. Russell, *Freshwater Recreational Fishing: The National Benefits of Water Pollution Control* (Resources for the Future, Washington, D.C. 1982).

3. The Keystone Center is a neutral nonprofit organization devoted to public policy and conflict management, particularly in the environmental area. The Center coordinates policy dialogues in which high-level representatives from business, environmental and citizen groups, research institutions, labor, and government gather to seek consensus and generate policy recommendations.